CONTENTS

Play Better Baseball

Winning Techniques and Strategies for Coaches and Players

BOB CLUCK

CONTEMPORARY BOOKS

A TRIBUNE COMPANY

Library of Congress Cataloging-in-Publication Data

Cluck, Bob.
    Play better baseball : winning techniques and strategies for
coaches and players / Bob Cluck.
       p.   cm.
   ISBN 0-8092-3922-1
   1. Baseball—Coaching.   I. Title.
GV875.5.C58   1993   92-37347
796.357'07'7—dc20   CIP

Published by Contemporary Books
An imprint of NTC/Contemporary Publishing Company
Two Prudential Plaza, Chicago, Illinois 60601-6790
Manufactured in the United States of America
International Standard Book Number: 0-8092-3922-1

ACKNOWLEDGMENTS

I wish to thank some of the people who share my interest in the game of baseball. In the beginning, Joe Schloss and Bill Whitaker, my Little League coaches, and my dad, Al Cluck, taught me about the game. Jerry Dahms, Bernie Flaherty, Ed San Clemente, and Mark Whitleton taught me how to compete, and Lyle Olsen turned me on to the mechanics and teaching of the game.

The San Diego School of Baseball gave me the opportunity to develop my teaching skills. Roger Craig and Bob Skinner taught me more about baseball than they realize. Together we developed "the nation's number-one baseball school," where thousands of players of all ages are taught to be better players. My other partners—Alan Trammell, Reggie Waller, Brent Strom, Tony Gwynn, Glenn Ezell, and Dave Smith—are wonderful business partners, great baseball men, and good friends.

In professional baseball, many people took an interest in me and gave me opportunities to become a good instructor. Dave Garcia signed me when nobody else would. Tal Smith gave me my first coaching job; Lynwood Stallings saved my job. Bill Wood is a great baseball man, the most honest person I know, and has had a great influence on me. I thank Bob Lillis and Tony Pacheco, who taught me how to teach, and Art Howe, who believed in me and gave me a chance in the major leagues.

My wife, Teri, who is not only a great photographer but a great wife and mother, and my daughters, Jennifer and Amber, who have grown up as real baseball kids, and my mother, Nina, the world's greatest Astros fan, have given me lots of support over the years.

1
COACHING BASEBALL AT ALL LEVELS

DEVELOPING WINNING PLAYERS

The value of sport in our society is immeasurable. Winning is a relative term normally used to describe the success of a team. It is easy for a coach to develop a healthy atmosphere on a winning team—the real challenge in coaching is teaching players how to cope with the tough times. Failure is a natural part of the game of baseball—the best teams lose 40 percent of their games; the best hitters fail nearly 70 percent of the time. Players who can't cope with the failure usually cannot survive at the higher levels of baseball. In society, people who don't develop these skills by playing sports or by other means generally don't compete well with others in business, school, and other areas of life.

I disagree with those who put down coaches in youth sports who think that winning is important. Winning is better than losing. Learning to beat your opponent in a fair, aggressive manner is not only important but is an absolute necessity. Show me a player who accepts losing too gracefully, and I'll show you a player who cannot produce when the game is on the line. Losing can become a very nasty habit—in baseball and in life.

When the winning becomes an obsession, the coach has

forgotten why he got into coaching in the first place. Coaches who put too much emphasis on winning and not enough on caring for their players miss the whole point of working with young people.

Athletes must understand that they are role models for younger people and have a responsibility to act accordingly. This might be the most important thing that coaches should teach players at all levels of the game.

DEALING WITH UMPIRES

In professional baseball and at the higher levels of amateur baseball umpires generally do a fine job. Umpires, players, and coaches need to work together to provide the fans with a fast-paced, entertaining game. Coaches who constantly get on umpires for little things are missing one important point: fans don't attend games to watch coaches coach. The old saying that when umpires do their best job they usually go unnoticed also is true for coaches. The fans and media only notice when umpires or coaches make mistakes.

Players will take on their coach's personality. If coaches abuse umpires, so will their players. Players should be taught to stand up for themselves—but not at the expense of professionalism.

DEALING WITH PARENTS AND OTHERS

In college and professional baseball, parents are not very visible. Only on rare occasions have I seen parents hinder the career of a player; most are supportive in every way.

In high school baseball, parents can be a big asset or a big pain. The average player who survives youth baseball may experience his first real failure at the high school level. When a player doesn't play regularly or gets cut from the team for the first time, he and his parents can become frustrated, and the coach can become an outlet for this anger. The coach is not always right but *is* entitled to his opinion, and he has a tough job making decisions on players. A player who loves the game and loves to play should never quit. I know of a few players who were cut from varsity and even junior varsity ball clubs and yet wound up playing professional baseball.

USING VIDEOTAPE AND HIGH-SPEED FILM

High-speed film and tape is an absolute necessity for studying baseball mechanics—a coach or instructor can use these and other aids to illustrate important points to players. But always review the film or tape prior to showing it to them. In fact, coaches using film or tape with players should follow this sequence:

1. Look at the film alone and identify the problem areas.
2. Design a plan of attack and a drill to correct the problem.
3. Introduce the drill while explaining the problem to the player.
4. After some progress, show the player the video.
5. Return to the drills until problem is solved.

Note: Do not let players look at negative video too often; instead, emphasize visualizing good mechanics. As a major league coach I seldom watch film with players unless I want to show a specific thing. Players see *too much* when they look at video. They try to fix things that aren't broken. This creates *new* problem areas.

The biggest fallacy regarding film or tape is that you simply film a hitter or pitcher when things are going bad and compare that with film when things are going good, and bingo—the differences will jump out at you. Unfortunately, it is just not that easy. Many times mechanical problems are undetectable, even with stop-action tape at one-thirtieth of a second. If you shot two tapes at different angles or with different technology, you might be misled by comparing the two films.

I have probably looked at more feet of video and tape than any coach or instructor alive, and the truth is that although video has many uses, it is simply not a cure-all for mechanical problems.

USING PRACTICE TIME EFFICIENTLY

A short, effective practice should be the goal of every coach. To accomplish this, coaches must structure practices following certain guidelines:

1. Keep the practice to 90 minutes or less.
2. Be specific about what you want to accomplish.

3. Be organized and have the field set up when the players arrive.
4. Explain to the players what you expect from them.
5. Tie in instruction with game situations.
6. Stay positive and upbeat and let the players have fun.

The availability of practice facilities and equipment will vary greatly. Some coaches will have three assistants, batting cages, pitching machines, batting tees, videotape equipment, protective screens, etc. Others will have next to nothing in the way of equipment. The key is to improvise and work with what is available. Good coaches find a way to teach baseball, prepare a team, and have fun at the same time.

Most practices involve batting practice and some form of defensive work. I suggest that you run your batting practice by time and not by number of swings. It is also a good idea to incorporate some baserunning drills into every practice. A system using stations is the most effective way to get a lot done in a short period of time. You simply divide the team into four groups: group one bats, group two runs the bases and reacts to the ball off the bat, group three takes ground balls and fly balls, and group four shags the balls from the hitters and helps the coach hit grounders and flies to group three. The groups rotate to the next station every 10 minutes. After 10 minutes of stretching, this part of the practice lasts 40 minutes, followed by a 40-minute scrimmage.

You can change the stations from time to time to work in specific fundamentals and keep the players interested. Whatever system you use, you should *never* hold a boring two-hour batting practice with a coach throwing one strike every four pitches. The kids will hate to come to practice unless you create a fun environment.

The Effective 90-Minute Practice

- 10 minutes—stretch and warm-up
- 40 minutes—station workout:
  Group 1—Hitting
  Group 2—Baserunning
  Group 3—Fielding

Group 4—Shagging and assisting coach
- 40 minutes—game situations or scrimmage

HOW TO USE YOUR OFFENSE

Getting on Base and Advancing Runners

In order for hitters to do their jobs properly, they must first recognize the game situation. The coach or manager of a team has the responsibility to teach players about game situations and how they change as the game progresses.

In baseball it is universally understood that the team that scores first has a distinct advantage. From the time the first hitter steps into the box to begin the game, every player on the team should be watching what the pitcher throws to start off each hitter, what he throws when behind the count or ahead in the count, and what his best pitch is. Hitters who are properly prepared mentally and physically have a better chance of getting on base.

Once a player gets on base, the goal is to move him into scoring position (second base). There are several ways to accomplish this: you can bunt the runner to second, you can have the runner steal the base, or you can use the hit-and-run. Nothing is more important to a team than the ability to move runners. The team that sits back and waits for extra-base hits or advances base to base usually loses the game. Whenever the coach can somehow advance a runner to third base with one out, or at least a runner to second with two outs, it takes just one hit to score. Baseball is a game of percentages, and the percentages are greatly against getting two hits in a row with two outs.

As a coach or manager, you are lucky to have several players in your lineup who have a good idea of the strike zone, which allows them to work for walks, or are able to bunt for a base hit. However, it is imperative that the entire team is able to execute the hit-and-run on both ends—that is, as hitters and as baserunners. The hit-and-run is one of the real keys to having an offense that can put runs on the board game after game. Sacrifice bunting has its place, but it costs you one of your precious 27 outs. Stealing a base is great, but you don't always have the people on the bases to accomplish this. Unless a team has vastly superior talent, it is a must that players understand the importance of advancing runners.

The hit-and-run does not require the runner to be fast, and most players can become proficient at handling the bat. Hitters must practice hitting down on the ball and keeping it on the ground. It takes terrific skill to hit behind the runner, and a coach should be satisfied if batters hit the ball anywhere on the ground. The play also opens up the defense, and many balls go through that would be outs without the movement on the bases. At the major league level, hitters do a terrible job practicing the hit-and-run—maybe they just don't believe in the importance of the play. Even in batting practice the baserunners rarely work on reacting to the ball. It may sound funny, but many college teams execute the hit-and-run better than most major league teams. Why, you ask? Because they believe in it and practice it correctly.

With a runner on second base and no outs, the batter *must* try to move the runner over to third—there are lots of ways for a runner to score from third with less than two outs. Some hitters wait for a pitch to hit toward second base; others work hard to become proficient at hitting the fastball the other way. Another option is to push a bunt toward second base. *If the hitter makes the second baseman or first baseman field the ball, the runner will be able to advance to third base with ease.* A coach should teach this kind of unselfish team play to all the players on his team. A player might get a 4-3 in the scorebook and an 0-for-1, but he will make a big impression on his coach and his teammates. Many players in professional baseball and some big stars in the major leagues are selfish and will never give themselves up for the benefit of the team. Fans and others may not notice this kind of play, but other players, coaches, and front-office people see these players for who they are.

Scoring a Runner from Third Base

When a runner is on third with less than two outs, the score will dictate where the defense is playing. If the infield is playing in to cut off the run at the plate, the runner on third must either wait for the ball to get through the infield or go "on contact." The contact play is used throughout the higher levels of baseball and is a must for every coach's game plan. The runner must get an aggressive lead (as far from the bag as the third baseman is) and simply go on contact. If the batter hits a hard grounder right at an infielder, the runner will probably be thrown out at the plate—but that is a chance the manager or coach takes. If the play is not on, the runner waits until the ball goes into the outfield before breaking for the plate. He must learn to freeze on line drives and break back on fly balls. He also should remember to tag up on all foul fly balls and watch for wild pitches on passed balls.

When the infield is back (giving up a run), the hitter can get the run in simply by hitting a grounder up the middle to shortstop or second base. Depending on the score, most teams will give up a run if they are way ahead and are playing for outs. Although this sounds easy you'd be surprised how many hitters in professional baseball fail to do it.

The squeeze and double steal are other alternatives for scoring a runner from third. Many coaches try to use these plays without practicing them enough and achieving the timing necessary to make them work. *On the squeeze bunt, the runner on third must not break and the hitter must not show bunt until the pitcher's arm starts forward, or until the pitcher's stride foot hits (same timing).* If the squeeze is executed properly, there is no defense for it; this is why some managers or coaches really like the play. On the double steal of second and home, the runner on third is the key to the play. He must read the catcher's intentions and break immediately when he releases the ball to second. If a trick defense is on, such as throwing back to the pitcher or to the shortstop or second baseman (called the "crash play"), the runner will probably be out—again, that is the chance you take on any aggressive offensive play. The runner stealing second should stop and get into a rundown if necessary to avoid running into the tag (if he is tagged out for the third out before the run scores, the run doesn't count).

GENERAL DEFENSIVE POSITIONING

In the major leagues, advance scouts supply detailed reports that enable the manager and his coaches to position their players properly. Hitters have certain well-established tendencies, and the overall defense should reflect these tendencies. *But the game situation will always override any predetermined positioning by the coaching staff.* Even in the majors, some coaches overreact to the scouting reports and forget that pitchers don't always throw the ball where they intend to. Although positioning is important with some hitters, as the old saying goes, "when in doubt, play them straight up": that is, position the infielders and the outfielders in the middle of their areas of responsibilities (refer to the infield and outfield chapters for details).

Late in the game, the defensive philosophy changes depending on the score. In a close game, the coach or manager may elect to have the third baseman and first baseman guard the lines to help prevent extra-base hits. The coach may also elect to play the outfield a little deeper from the seventh inning on to avoid an extra-base hit when the game is close.

Deciding when to play the infield in to cut off a run is always a tough one for a coach or manager. ("In" refers to the infielders positioning themselves in the baseline or one step either way depending on the speed of the runner at third.) The rule of thumb is that when you think that the run represented on third may ultimately beat you, play the infield in. If you are facing a very tough pitcher and you think that runs will be tough to come by, you may want to bring the infield in early in the game so as not to fall too far behind.

With runners on first and third with one out, the coach may elect to play the first and third basemen in to cut off the run but play the shortstop and second baseman back in double-play depth to end the inning with a double play.

THE PSYCHOLOGY OF COACHING

Sports psychologists talking about Little League or other youth sports say things like "Let them have fun" or "Give the game back to the kids." In the major leagues and every level of baseball the same thing is true. When big-league players in a recent World Series were asked why their managers were successful, the majority said, "We have fun" and "He lets the players play." At all levels of baseball, the most important thing for a coach to promote is fun. Every coach or manager must be very flexible in his approach. All players are not alike, and the coach who treats everybody the same will miss on some of the players. I've managed at the Class-A and Triple-A levels and I've coached in the major leagues, and I have found that players want rules and structure. If you are fair in your overall approach, they will respect your rules and abide by them. However, a coach with too many rules will end up disciplining players more and coaching and teaching them less.

Establishing Goals

Athletes often have difficulty setting the right kind of short-term and long-term goals. Short-term goals should be fairly specific: "hit the ball the other way more often," for example, or "throw first-pitch strikes" are much more useful than "I want to have a good game." Goals should also be realistic: athletes who set goals like "I want to hit four home runs" or "I want to throw a perfect game" will most times end up disappointed and discouraged. It is a good idea for players to put their goals in writing and refer to them occasionally.

Coaches should help players set their goals and, more important, suggest ways in which they might attain them. If a hitter's short-term goal is to "hit the ball the other way more often," then the coach's responsibility is to teach the player hitting skills that will enable him to succeed at this task. A coach should periodically discuss players' short- and long-term goals and make adjustments—goals need be constantly revised and updated to keep players motivated.

Players who set goals that are too low, or perhaps set no goals at all, are expecting too little from themselves—and, believe me, that is what they are likely to get. If a coach sets goals for his team and individual players that are too low, chances are he will have a team full of mediocre, complacent players. I have heard major league managers say things like "just show up on time and play hard." Those kind of expectations are too vague and promote average play from players. "Play hard" means different things to different players. Players at all levels must be told specifically what is expected of them on an almost daily—or at least a weekly—basis in order to get the most out of their abilities.

Accepting Responsibility

Players from Little League to the majors are looking for excuses for why they fail: they blame the wind, the sun, the umpire, their teammates, or just "rotten luck." Players who do not accept responsibility for a missed throw, a baserunning mistake, or a base on balls have no reason to try to improve; in their minds, someone *else* should work harder to improve *their* game. Compulsive "responsibility dodgers" blame their teachers for poor grades and their bosses for getting fired from their jobs. Some people are burdened by this attitude for a lifetime.

One of the most important lessons that coaches must teach their athletes is to accept responsibility for their own actions. A coach who neglects this area has failed as a coach.

Mental Preparation

The average professional baseball player is not mentally prepared to cope with a 200-game schedule (counting spring training). If a coach asked most major leaguers what terms such as concentration, visualization, self-talk, or relaxation meant to them, he would get answers that would surprise a high school psychology teacher. *The sad truth is that most baseball players—and some coaches— don't think that mental training is as important as physical training.* Coaches shout "Concentrate on the ball!" or "Throw strikes!" yet haven't taught players how to concentrate or improve control. They leave them mentally stranded to fend for themselves and to figure out a way to succeed. Players in this situation must learn mental training on their own through a "destined for failure, trial and error" method. Many times *players not only don't do anything to help themselves but may use techniques such as negative self- talk and visualization to turn in poorer overall performances.*

Concentration The art of concentration can be the simplest thing in the world: if you are interested in what you are doing, concentrating on that subject is easy. A coach who promotes an atmosphere of fun will find that players get into baseball and start learning and succeeding at a faster rate.

Concentration is especially important with difficult skills such as throwing or hitting a baseball. Everyone has had the experience of reading a page in a book and then not being able to recall anything he had just read. This is an example of poor concentration: the mind was focused on something, but not on the book.

Lack of concentration can turn a potential superstar into a mediocre athlete; the ability to control concentration can enable an athlete with average physical abilities to excel.

During a game, a player hears and sees many things in the stands and on the field; in addition, he is probably thinking about earlier plays as well as possible future game situations. It can be a struggle to remain centered only on the present and not let the mind wander from the task at hand. One very effective way to accomplish this is by a concentration technique known as "fine centering": focusing one's eyes or channeling one's attention toward a small area. The focused area can be the catcher's glove, the pitcher's release point, or any spot the player chooses—the important thing is that fine centering on a target causes everything else to blur and fade away; that's what concentration is all about.

Coaches should encourage fine centering by giving very specific instructions to players. For example, when a coach shouts advice like "Throw strikes!" or "Get a base hit!" players probably don't hear anything he says. On the other hand, specific tips like "See the catcher's glove and throw through it" or "See the ball at the release point—try to see it clearly" are more likely to get better results.

Relaxation techniques Everybody is uptight when facing an exam, going on a date, speaking in public, or playing a game in front of people. The coach and the player must recognize the symptoms of abnormal tension and anxiety and why people display these symptoms. A coach can tell instantly if a player is nervous by counting his breaths per minute (unless he just scored from first on a double). Another method I use is placing my hand on the player's shoulder—if he is abnormally nervous, he will feel very tight in this area.

When I feel this tension or see abnormal breathing patterns, I suggest positive self-talk or positive visualization—this usually does the trick. The last thing the player needs at this point is for the coach or anyone else to say "Don't walk this guy" or "Don't strike out" or anything that puts more pressure on him. I also use humor to relax players. My feeling is that when a player takes the game or himself too seriously, this affects his performance in a negative way.

Athletes display no more nervousness than anyone else. *Some amount of arousal is not only normal but absolutely necessary to perform at an optimal level.* Some athletes describe it as being "psyched" or "pumped"—everyone feels these emotions before and during any athletic contest. When an athlete learns to regulate this arousal, these positive feelings and emotions will help him perform to the maximum in all situations.

Many of the problems associated with nervousness are closely connected with breathing levels before and during competition. A technique called cardiac deceleration is helping many athletes relax and perform at a higher level. Dr. Fran Pirozzolo of the Astros and Baylor College of Medicine has done substantial work in this area. An Astros pitcher was measured at 52 breaths per minute at one point in the first two innings of his major league debut. With the heart racing as it would when breathing is at that level, any pitcher would have difficulty seeing his target and delivering the ball with consistency. By stepping behind the mound, taking two deep breaths, and centering on the task at hand (the pitch he was going to throw and the target), he was able to slow his breathing to 35 breaths per minute in his second game.

Visualization and self-talk Most players, like everyone else, have the ability to create vivid pictures in their minds. Self-talk helps create these pictures and has a profound effect on athletic performance. I think some baseball players try very hard to think in a positive way, but since baseball is a negative sport (an average hitter fails 75 percent of the time), it is easy for negative thoughts to creep into the program.

A reciprocal relationship seems to exist between positive and negative self-talk. In order to increase positive self-talk and decrease the amount of negative self-talk, you should (1) write down all the positive thoughts that specifically pertain to the task at hand; (2) lay down in a quiet place and read your positive thoughts over and over, painting vivid pictures in your mind of each thought; and (3) each time a negative thought enters your mind, think *No!* or some similar command and replace that negative thought with a positive one from your list.

You should use your imagination and not be afraid to ask for help from coaches, parents, and even other players. Your list should be very task-specific and refer exactly to the skill that you are trying to perform. For instance, a pitcher would include thoughts such as "I see my curveball breaking down at the knees, hitting the glove, and the umpire's right arm going up and calling it a strike," or "I'm throwing a fastball inside on the corner and I see the hitter swing and pop it straight up in the infield." Eventually the list should include nearly every situation and task pertaining to your position. The more detail that each image contains, the better (including things like crowd noise can be very helpful). These positive images will soon be easy to recall, and the negative self-talk and visualization for the most part will be eliminated.

A positive attitude Confidence takes time. Every player has doubts about his performance until his track record has been established. When players are facing a new level of competition for the first time, those doubts are always present. Pitchers, for example, at the Class AA level who are very aggressive, challenge hitters, and throw lots of strikes suddenly become tentative and try to "miss bats" rather than challenge hitters when they are moved up to Class AAA. Then, when they are sent back down (after failing at Triple A and with no other changes), they instantly become aggressive again and throw nothing but strikes. *Until the player realizes that the players at the next level are not supermen but ballplayers like him, he can't succeed.* The myth exists among minor leaguers and others that major league hitters hit every fastball over the plate hard and that pitchers all throw 90 miles per hour. The truth, for the most part, is that the physical skills in the high minors are the same as in the big leagues. The difference is that many major leaguers have better mental skills—in other words, they can "handle the action."

Telling a player to think positive is very fashionable, but it is not very effective unless your instructions are very specific. Players must learn to develop the skills necessary to think positively. *Positive thinking is nothing more than positive self-talk leading to positive visualization.* According to Dr. Pirozzolo, "Positive self-talk works by replacing the mind's negative, anxiety-provoking chatter with positive, constructive statements that are evoked automatically during stressful situations." Only by writing the positive thoughts down on paper and repeating them to yourself regularly can you evoke these thoughts automatically. Dr. Pirozzolo suggests that you

- keep your thoughts focused in the present
- keep your thoughts focused on things you can control
- separate your performance from your self-worth (if you fail, you're not a bad person)
- remember that mistakes are natural occurrences and learn from them

The following are some examples of "positive affirmations." A coach should discuss these items one at a time and understand that each one will mean something a little different to each player.

- I will do my best to become the best that I am capable of becoming.
- I am a worthy and capable human being regardless of how I perform on the field.
- I am not responsible for other people's actions, but I take complete responsibility for myself and my actions.
- I am willing to let go of all the negative, limiting, and unproductive thoughts I have thought before.
- I forgive myself for all mistakes and offenses, for I am human and everyone makes mistakes.
- I will use more and more of myself until I eventually reach a much fuller range of my potential.
- I will not compare myself to other people, for no two people have the same level of ability or experience.
- I will concentrate on doing my best right now because I cannot change what has happened in the past.
- I recognize that every challenge is an opportunity to take a positive step toward reaching my potential.

2
PITCHING: THE FOUNDATION OF EVERY TEAM

WHAT DOES IT TAKE TO BECOME A WINNING PITCHER?

Young pitchers, their coaches, their parents, college coaches, and pro scouts put too much emphasis on velocity. Pitchers who try to throw with more velocity than they are capable of generating open up too soon, destroy their mechanics, and become inefficient. They are inviting arm injuries.

It's nice to have pitchers with great arms, but many winning pitchers in the big leagues have below-average major league fastballs. During a recent major league season, all pitchers were timed with radar guns, and it was found that fewer than 10 had the kind of velocity to put them in the "power" class. In fact, the average for all major league pitchers was 84 miles per hour. Velocity can help a player get signed or get a college scholarship, but smart coaches want one kind of pitcher: one who wins.

A winning pitcher

- Develops a good delivery at an early age
- Develops a fastball with movement
- Has a breaking pitch that he can control
- Throws a change-up with hand speed that fools the hitter

- Pitches inside on a regular basis
- Learns how to use his pitches to get people out
- Fields his position well and backs up bases
- Holds runners well
- Recognizes game situations and pitches accordingly
- Takes care of his arm
- Is serious about weight training, conditioning, and nutrition
- Does not blame his losses on umpires, catchers, or other teammates

PITCHING MECHANICS

In 1970 Roger Craig and I started the San Diego School of Baseball. The school soon became a university for baseball instructors: pitchers and pitching coaches such as Brent Strom, Don Alexander, Mark Lee, Gary Lucas, Dave Smith, Randy Jones, Bob Miller, and Tom House would join Roger and me for hours before and after classes to talk about pitching. A new way of teaching pitching mechanics was developed by research and the exchange of ideas. Roger was the guru, but we all contributed and learned from one other. We developed, among other things, the split-fingered fastball, which has forever changed the way the battle between hitter and pitcher is fought.

I have taught throwing and pitching mechanics to students from ages 6 to 22 at the San Diego School of Baseball, and I have taught major leaguers as a coach for the Houston Astros. One thing that has become increasingly clear to me over the years is that pitching mechanics are the same for 6-year-olds and major leaguers. The presentation of these mechanical fundamentals changes somewhat at each level, but the problems that beginners have are the same ones that major league superstars have.

The pitching mechanics presented in this chapter can be used for pitchers at every level, from Little League to professionals. Remember—mechanics always should be taught in a logical, sequential manner at a very slow pace.

The Three Phases of the Pitching Delivery

The pitching delivery can be divided into three phases: (1) from the initial stance up to and including the balance position (fig. 2-

2-1. The balanced position—
the first part of the delivery.

2-2. The arm is up, back, and ready to go
forward when the stride foot lands.

1); (2) from the balance position to when the stride foot lands (fig.
2-2); and (3) after the stride foot is down. *No further breakdown is
necessary to acquire an understanding of the delivery.* Pitching
problems at all levels can be diagnosed and treated through the use
of this simple three-part breakdown of pitching mechanics.

When a coach is faced with a problem, many times he must
invent a solution using common sense. Once you acquire a base
knowledge of mechanics, you will be able to break down the
delivery, trace the problem to its root, and develop a drill to solve
the problem.

Getting to the balance point A pitcher should begin in a
comfortable stance, with weight equally distributed and the hands
in a relaxed position. When using a windup a pitcher can have his

2-3. Many pitchers start with their hands together in the windup position.

2-4. Some pitchers place the ball behind their back to start the windup.

2-5. Placing the ball in the glove helps to prevent a pitcher from tipping his pitches.

hands together (fig. 2-3) or apart (fig. 2-4), depending on personal preference. Either way, however, it is generally a good idea to start with the ball in the glove (fig. 2-5) rather than the pitching hand to avoid the possibility of tipping the pitch.

It is best to take a small step back (fig. 2-6); pitchers who take a large step back (fig. 2-7) often will have trouble keeping their balance. A key movement in reaching this extremely important

2-6. A small step back with the free foot is highly recommended.

2-7. A large step back may cause a loss of balance.

2-8. The balance point helps the pitcher collect his weight before starting forward.

2-9. When a pitcher kicks his free leg out, he may lean backward with the upper body and lose balance and direction to home plate.

balanced position (fig. 2-8) is the leg lift and body turn during the middle of the windup sequence. A pitcher should think "lift the knee to the chest" and *not* kick or swing the leg away from the body. Kicking the free leg away from the body will cause the upper body to lean back in an attempt to maintain balance (fig. 2-9). Throughout this phase of the delivery, the pitcher should be trying to keep his head very still and directly over his back foot.

Phase two Two important events should happen simultaneously during phase two of the pitching delivery: The pitching hand breaks from the glove, makes its semicircle, and arrives at what is called the loaded position (fig. 2-10), which is the pitching hand's highest point. At the same time, the stride leg has moved from the balance point (its highest position) and has been planted in the direction of home plate. These two movements take less than half a second; when they don't match—when there is an error in timing

2-10. The pitcher's arm should be up and back to its highest position when the stride foot hits—this is called the loaded position.

of just a few hundredths of a second—the pitcher's timing is destroyed and the results are bad.

Phase three Most of the effort involved in the pitching delivery kicks in during phase three. The stride foot has been planted, and the hand is ready to come forward; now the pitcher extends his hand toward the target and throws the ball in an all-out effort.

Legs, hips, and the "push" that doesn't exist The "drop and drive" theory was taught throughout baseball until the 1980s. Indeed, observing the likes of Nolan Ryan, Tom Seaver, or Roger Clemens still *seems* to confirm the notion that pitchers push off the rubber with their back leg and drive toward the plate. However, the truth is that teaching pitchers to push off the rubber just makes them rush their delivery and destroys their leverage and balance.

In the 1980s, researchers in Houston determined that Nolan Ryan applied very little pressure against the rubber with his back foot. Analysis of slow-motion film clearly shows that once a pitcher bends his back leg, he keeps that leg bent at an almost constant angle throughout the delivery. Common sense dictates that without extension, or straightening, of the back leg, not much leg drive can be generated. In other words, *pitchers don't push with their back legs at all—what people see is the back foot being "pulled" off the rubber by the violent action of the hips.* This is why pitching coaches have been confused for decades.

The hips open *after* the stride foot lands. Leg and trunk strength are very important to a pitcher's delivery: the faster he can rotate his hips and trunk, the faster his backside can get through. If a pitcher is mechanically sound, strong legs and a strong abdominal region can greatly increase hand speed and therefore velocity.

Rushing—the mechanical monster Rushing during the stride (phase two) is by far the biggest culprit in the breakdown of pitching mechanics at all levels. The reason for this is very simple:

2-11. This pitcher's weight is going forward before the free leg gets to its highest point— a sure sign of rushing.

the pitcher is trying to throw too hard by making the stride a powerful movement. If the stride foot hits before the pitching hand arrives at the loaded position, then the ball will be brought forward from that slightly lower position, resulting in a loss of leverage. He is now throwing "uphill." Because the pitcher's elbow is below shoulder height, everyone tells him to get his elbow up, but the root of the problem is rushing. The pitcher should think of his front side as directional only and his backside as the power side. In reality, the backside "pushes" the front side out of the way even more than the front side "pulls" the backside through.

To summarize: A pitcher must maintain his weight over his back foot until his front knee gets to its highest point (the balance point). *If he starts his weight forward toward the plate before he reaches this point (fig. 2-11), the timing of his entire delivery is destroyed.* If he reaches the balance point properly (fig. 2-12), he can split his hands (fig. 2-13), start his stride (fig. 2-14), and transfer his weight forward with a normal delivery (fig. 2-15).

2-12. Keeping the head over the back leg until the leg gets to its highest point will maintain balance and increase the chance for good direction.

2-13. When the pitcher starts forward he splits his hands but keeps his head on line to the plate.

2-14. The stride starts—the pitcher should be concentrating on direction and balance.

2-15. The pitcher completes the weight transfer and releases the ball with his head out over his front knee.

THE PITCHES: TOOLS TO GET HITTERS OUT

Control of the Fastball

The foundation for every pitcher is his fastball. Whether it's used to overpower hitters (which is very rarely the case) or to set up other pitches, the fastball is the key to successful pitching. And the keys to developing an effective fastball are control and movement. Young pitchers think that velocity is the most important factor, but this kind of thinking leads to overthrowing, one of the pitching coach's biggest enemies. Overthrowing is a career-long problem: it can never be completely overcome, but it can be controlled. Even the best major league pitchers overthrow in some situations.

Pitching Inside

Pitchers have to pitch inside to be effective. There are three basic inside pitches at the major league level. The first is thrown on the corner. The second is thrown three to four inches off the plate in an effort to jam, or tie up, the hitter and get him out. The third, called the purpose pitch, is thrown at the hitter's hands, and its message is simple: *move or get hit*. The purpose pitch should never be higher than letter high or lower than belt high. A pitcher must protect the outside half of the plate by discouraging the hitter from leaning out over the plate. Pitching inside should be a regular part of a pitcher's plan and not be a display of frustration or a malicious act. Trying to hit somebody shows a lack of character. However, pitchers in the major leagues today don't pitch inside like they used to. I wish I could figure out why. . . .

The Four-Seam Fastball

Pitchers usually develop a four-seam (or cross-seam) fastball at an early age. It is the fastball that some will rely on throughout their pitching careers. The basic grip (fig. 2-16), held dead center, provides for little movement. However, moving the fingers off-center to the left (fig. 2-17) will make the ball run right and even sink when thrown down around the knees by a right-handed pitcher. When held off-center to the right (fig. 2-18), the ball will break left, or cut in, toward a left-handed hitter from a right-handed pitcher. (Note: when the fastball is thrown off-center it is advisable to place the fingers together on the ball.)

The four-seam fastball can be used as a foundation grip for many other pitches. It is also an essential tool for teaching pitchers how spin affects the flight of the ball.

2-16. The cross-seam, or four-seam, grip provides for true flight and maximum velocity of the fastball.

2-17. For a left-hander this grip will make the ball run in on right-handed hitters.

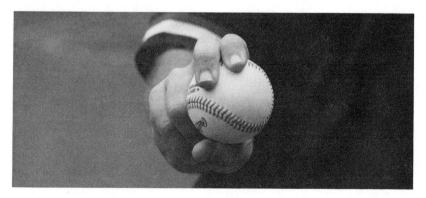

2-18. Holding the ball off-center in the other direction makes the ball run away from a right-handed hitter and in on a left-handed hitter.

The Two-Seam Grip and the Sinker

The two-seam fastball (also called "with-the-seams") (fig. 2-19) provides for the best movement among the fastball grips. Generally, most sliders and sinkers also come from this grip by holding the ball off-center.

The sinker is a two-seam fastball that has been held off-center. Many different grips have been used successfully, but the grip that I have found to be the best is the with-the-seams fastball with the middle finger "hooking" the seam (fig. 2-20). The sinker can also be thrown across the two seams (fig. 2-21) and will

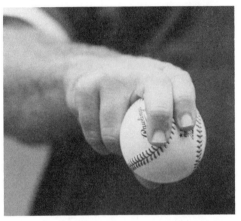

2-19. A popular grip for the sinker is the two-seam fastball grip with pressure on the middle finger.

2-20. Hooking a seam makes the ball sink more sharply, and when the pitcher gets the ball up it will still run, giving the pitch more margin for error.

2-21. An alternate grip for the sinker: placing the fingers across two seams.

generally get the same spin and the same results. The thumb also plays an important role in this sinker grip: by sliding the thumb up the side of the ball or by tucking it underneath, the pitcher isolates the pressure to the middle finger and creates tighter spin.

Choice of grip should be based on comfort and personal preference for the pitcher. A pitching coach should encourage pitchers to try lots of grips during their careers. As the size of a pitcher's hands change or his grip strength improves, different grips will provide variations of spin and movement. The bottom line on the sinker is that the grip should do the work. The pitcher shouldn't try to help the sinker by trying to force his hand to the inside while releasing the ball. This process will inhibit the spin and provide for a "soft" sinker (a sinker with a slow break). In order to get the sharpest break, the pitcher should set the grip and think "throw a fastball." Only when a pitcher has substantial hand speed will the sinker produce the desired results—lots of ground balls.

The Split-Fingered Fastball

The split-fingered fastball became popular in the early 1980s. It was never meant to be a power pitch, but pitchers started pushing the ball farther and farther between their fingers, and this devastating pitch was born. Cy Young Award winner Mike Scott took the pitch to the extreme and threw it very hard with great movement. At the apex of his career, Scott was throwing the split 85–88 miles per hour and the bottom was falling out of it. This was not the purpose of the split. It was meant from the beginning to be a super change-up that is easy to learn and easy to control—*not* a power pitch.

The split has saved careers like no other pitch in history. In 1976, I signed Dave Smith to a contract with the Houston Astros and sent him to rookie league. Dave had a good arm, but his career proceeded slowly. He pitched well at times but never had a winning record in the minors, and his chances of making the majors were slim. He added the split in 1979, and after a stint in Puerto Rico playing winter ball the pitch was ready for major league hitters. He made the big club in 1980 and saved more than 200 games, becoming one of the game's best relievers. His success can be traced to the split and a *very* competitive spirit.

At the San Diego School of Baseball in the late 1970s, Roger Craig and I began experimenting with what we called a "split-fingered change-up": a pitch designed to keep youngsters from throwing breaking balls too early. The fingers were split just slightly (see "Changing Speeds") to give the pitcher an easy change-up to throw. In the next few years, we tried it on older kids who came to our winter camps. When it worked so well for them, Roger took it to Detroit, where he became pitching coach in 1982, and it took off from there. The Detroit Tigers won the World Series in 1984, and the split-fingered fastball played a major role in their success.

The split-fingered fastball is held with the fingers split on the outside of the seams of a with-the-seam fastball grip (fig 2-22). Some pitchers prefer to hook a seam with their middle finger to give the pitch a different spin (fig. 2-23). The split-finger is thrown just like a fastball, which is why it is so easy to learn. *It is imperative that the wrist be flexible.* Pitchers *must not* place the ball too far down between the fingers (fig. 2-24). This type of grip inhibits the flexibility of the wrist and results in a pitch that won't spin properly; it also can lead to serious elbow damage.

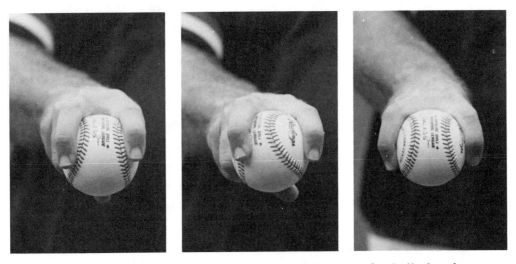

2-22. This is the basic grip for the split-fingered fastball that has revolutionized pitching since the mid-1980s. This pitch is used primarily as a change-up.

2-23. Some pitchers prefer to hook a seam with one finger or the other.

2-24. When the fingers are split too far, wrist movement is restricted and an elbow injury is very possible.

The split-fingered fastball has gotten a bad rap from some uninformed baseball people. Unless it is jammed way down between the fingers and inhibits wrist movement, it is simply not dangerous. With supervision, the pitch can be thrown by pitchers of all ages.

Sliders and Cutters

Since the 1980s, the slider has been more popular than the curve-ball among pitchers signing pro contracts. Since the curve takes more time to develop properly, lots of college pitchers take to the slider for quicker results.

The slider is actually a fastball cut in the opposite direction of the sinker. For decades, the rap on the slider has been that it causes arm problems. When thrown properly, the slider should not cause any more problems than any other pitch. Many young pitchers fall in love with the slider and overthrow it. In extreme cases, I have seen college pitchers throw 70 percent sliders. Pitchers should throw a maximum of 30 percent breaking pitches as a rule of thumb.

Most baseball people don't understand the relationship between the slider and its brother the cut fastball, or cutter. A cutter should move across a relatively flat plane from right to left (from a right-handed pitcher) and should be thrown belt high or above. Right-handed pitchers will throw a cutter belt high and in off the plate to a left-handed hitter in an effort to tie him up, or jam him. The right-hander will also throw the cutter up and away to a right-handed hitter to entice the hitter to chase the ball out of the strike zone (see "Calling Your Own Game"). When pitchers throw a cutter down by the knees it sometimes will break a short distance (6 to 10 inches) like a slider.

There are several popular grips for the slider (figs. 2-25, 2-26, and 2-27); as long as the middle finger acts as a pressure point, almost any grip will work. The thought process is really the key issue with the slider. The pitcher must think "cut the ball" and not "I'm throwing a breaking ball." When the pitcher thinks "breaking ball," he will come around the ball and twist it on the end (fig. 2-28). *This is the primary cause for elbow problems associated with the slider.* A true slider has a short break when thrown down in the

2-25, 2-26, and 2-27. These are all popular grips for the slider. The pitcher should think "Cut the ball" and not "Twist the wrist."

2-28. This twisting action on a slider can cause major elbow problems.

strike zone. If the break is bigger than 6 to 10 inches, you can assume that the pitcher is twisting the ball on the end. If thinking "cut the ball" doesn't shorten the break, the pitching coach has no choice but to take the slider away from the pitcher—especially if any arm problems have surfaced. Arm problems are very predictable for a pitcher who twists his slider. This twisting slider, or "slurve" (half slider and half curve), is thrown hard, and the twisting action goes against *pronation*, the natural movement of the hand (after releasing the ball, the hand turns inside out). Slurves are very popular because they are effective at the lower levels of baseball. In my opinion, this pitch will damage the elbow eventually—a properly thrown slider or a curveball is a much better alternative for a safer breaking pitch.

I have taken the slurve away from pitchers in the minor leagues. Since it is often the pitcher's favorite pitch, this is not a popular move: here is a guy fighting for his life, and you are telling him that he can't throw his favorite—and most effective—pitch. One of the reasons why Bill Wood, Astros general manager, hired me in 1989 was to find out why many of the Astros' pitching prospects had gone down to arm injuries. It was obvious to me that the slurve was a major part of the overall problem. After taking away the slurves, we tried to teach pitching prospects to throw curveballs instead. All of them developed great curveballs, and after they made it to the majors we let them throw a properly thrown slider on a limited basis. They all have their favorite pitches back now (along with a great curve that they never would have developed), and they like me again.

The Curveball ("Uncle Charlie," "The Hook")

Fathers and coaches tell us, "I don't allow my pitchers to throw curves yet," but the kids are throwing them on the playground anyway. Kids start spinning the ball at an early age and in most cases twist off sidearm curves in order to see the ball break. They quickly learn that this side-to-side break is very effective (right-handed pitcher versus right-handed hitter). But pitchers who throw side-to-side curveballs in Little League and are big winners are often not around to enjoy the same success in high school. Twisting the wrist and creating this side-to-side spin (fig. 2-29) probably has caused more arm problems than anything else.

Ever since Candy Cummings threw the first curveball in the 1860s, people have been trying to explain why curves break. Much like an airplane wing in reverse, differences in air pressure on the top and the bottom of the ball pull the curveball down. (The reason is probably due more to the Magnus Effect, but I'll leave that debate to the physicists.) Through the efforts of Robert K. Adair (*The Physics of Baseball*), Peter Brancazio (*Sport Science*), and others, baseball technicians have gained a deeper appreciation of their craft. Even a partial comprehension of drag coefficients and aerodynamics will help you understand how a baseball spins and breaks.

At the San Diego School of Baseball we believe that since kids are already spinning baseballs by age 10 or 11 they might as well learn to spin them correctly. *Young pitchers are going to throw a breaking pitch of some kind in order to compete, so why not teach them the proper way to throw it from the beginning?*

To throw the curveball properly a pitcher must first understand how the ball must spin. A properly thrown curveball is what some people call a "drop." The ball is held along the long seam in a manner to allow four seams to hit the wind while the ball is in flight (fig. 2-30). It is not necessary to try to make the ball drop

2-29. Kids learn to throw the sidearm curveball at an early age. This twisting action is very dangerous for young arms.

2-30. The four-seam curve is the basic major league curveball.

straight down. The break each pitcher gets will depend on his natural arm position. He should throw his curveball from the same arm position that he throws his fastball. Many pitchers have trouble with their curves because they lean back in order to artificially get "on top." When this happens, it slows hand speed, decreases spin, and impedes overall balance.

Pitchers must spend many hours learning to spin the ball to make it break down. They can throw 20 or 30 curves every other day on the side (throwing easy) until they are very comfortable with the grip and release of the ball. The process is long and tedious, but a good curveball is a devastating weapon against the hitter. *Considering all factors, coaches should make every effort to encourage the curve rather than the slider for young pitchers.* The slider should only be considered when it becomes clear that a pitcher simply cannot throw the curve. But be careful not to pull the plug on it too soon—a period of two months is sometimes required to gain *moderate* success with a curveball.

Changing Speeds

By far the most effective weapon the pitcher has against the hitter is the ability to change speeds on his pitches. Hitters look for the fastball on nearly every pitch—this is true in Little League, the major leagues, and every other level. They may see differences in the spin or the trajectory of pitches like the curve or slider, but the change of speed is the last thing they recognize. *Throwing a change-up is an absolute must for every pitcher at the higher levels.*

Hitters are fooled by the pitcher's hand speed (also referred to as arm speed) at the release point. If the pitcher shows the hitter fastball hand speed, he will start his swing to hit the fastball. In order to show the hitter the hand speed necessary to fool him, the pitcher must think "fastball" when he throws the change-up. Any effort to slow down the ball with the body or arm will slow hand speed and give away the pitch. *The grip must do 100 percent of the job of slowing the ball down to change-up speed.* Lots of pitchers worry too much about throwing the pitch too hard. The pitcher *should* feel as if he is throwing it too hard. Most major league change-ups are clocked at 8–10 miles per hour slower than the pitcher's fastball.

Several grips can be used for the change-up. There are basically three styles—the straight change, the screwball (yes, it is a change-up), and the split-fingered change. The straight change is very effective in making the hitter think he is swinging at a fastball—the spin on the ball is similar to that of the fastball. Again, the difference in speed ideally is 8–10 miles per hour, but some changes are effective with 12 or even 15 miles per hour off the fastball speed. *The foundation for all straight-change grips is placing the ball back into the palm of the hand (fig.2-31).*

The circle change is really half a screwball and is held back in the hand with the index finger touching the thumb (fig. 2-32). The

2-31. Every straight change is an offspring of the basic palmball grip.

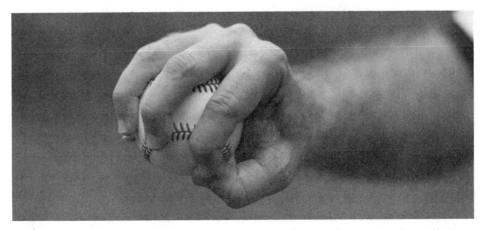

2-32. The circle change is turned over by the pitcher and spins a little like a screwball.

2-33. The most popular change-up is the three-fingered change, so named because the little finger is down the side of the ball and the thumb is underneath, leaving three fingers on top of the ball.

2-34. Screwball pitchers place the middle finger (sometimes the index finger) along a seam and rotate the ball counterclockwise (for a right-handed pitcher).

three-fingered change is also held back in the hand, but the index finger and the thumb don't touch (fig. 2-33).

The screwball is thrown with varying degrees of spin by major leaguers, although the true screwball is thrown by just a handful of active big-league pitchers. Anytime a pitcher uses forced pronation, or an inward turn of the hand, he is basically throwing a variation of a screwball. The ball is usually held along a seam (fig. 2-34), and the pitcher tries to "throw" the index finger over the top of the ball to create the spin. Most pitchers use the middle finger as the "power" finger, but I have seen one or two use the index finger to impart the spin.

The split-fingered change-up is thrown by splitting the fingers off of the with-the-seams fastball grip. It is important not to split the fingers so far that wrist movement becomes restricted. As long as the wrist remains as flexible as it does on the fastball, the split-fingered change should not hurt the pitcher's arm.

The development of these pitches takes time, and lots of young pitchers won't stay with a grip long enough for it to feel good. A pitcher should play catch using the grip almost daily, and a coach should insist that his young pitchers throw 20–30 percent changes in games until they see the results (pop-ups, weak ground outs, and strikeouts) and start to believe in the pitch.

The toughest job for a pitching coach is to sell the change-up to his pitchers. At first, they hate the concept of throwing their third- or fourth-best pitch to the hitter. In pro ball, a 2-0 or 3-1 fastball is your third- or fourth-best pitch. It becomes sort of a catch-22: "I can't throw my change for a strike so I don't use it" and "I don't use it because I can't throw it for a strike." You hear things like "I'll throw it in the next game." Before long, the season is over and it's "We'll have to work on it next year." *Young pitchers must be forced to throw it*. Call the pitches from the bench—make them throw it, even on the first pitch. Eventually, they will thank you when the pitch is helping them win games at the higher levels.

Here are a few reminders for pitchers trying to develop a change-up:

- Find a grip that is comfortable and stick with it—the grip does all the work.
- Hand speed is what fools the hitter.
- Movement is desirable, but not at the expense of hand speed.
- Don't pick corners—throw your change-up down the middle.
- Stay with it and it will help you win at the higher levels. (You didn't stop throwing your fastball just because it got hit once or twice.)

SETTING UP HITTERS: THE GAME WITHIN A GAME

A coach should never take for granted that a pitcher recognizes the game situation and will have a sound plan of attack. Pitchers get "lost" during games. Even major leaguers lose emotional control at times and have to be reminded to slow down, regain good mechanics, and stop overthrowing. Pitchers at all levels should be reminded of game situations during the heat of battle. I have gone to the mound to remind veteran pitchers that first base is open and to pitch around a tough hitter. It might seem silly, but *you never want to lose a game because you assumed something— Never!*

On a rare occasion, a pitching coach will go to the mound to discuss mechanics. Sometimes a coach might mention balance or direction but no new information should be offered during a game. Most of the time it is just a confidence builder or a break so the pitcher can think about the situation he is facing. A coach can try to break the tension when things are not going well or distract the pitcher from feeling sorry for himself. In a game at Cincinnati during the 1991 season, Astros pitcher Mark Portugal gave up three consecutive home runs on four pitches. At the Reds' ball-park, fireworks go off after each home run. I went to the mound and told him, "Mark, I came out to slow you down—the guy needs time to reload his cannon." Portugal and catcher Craig Biggio had a good laugh and then didn't give up another hit for five innings, and we won the game. Sometimes you have to dig deep for something to tell a pitcher to get him through the tough times.

Typical Game Situations—Late Innings of a Close Game

A leadoff hitter with very little power It should be obvious that this hitter will take some pitches and work the count. A leadoff walk would put the offense in a strong position, so this hitter is unlikely to swing at many bad pitches. Start with a fastball on the outside half of the plate for a strike. Staying ahead in the count is essential, so come back with another fastball on the inside or the outside half for strike two. You can take a shot at a bad breaking ball for strike three, but by all means come back with a strike on the fourth pitch. This kind of hitter must be made to swing the bat. The possibility of a bunt for a hit exists, so make sure the first and third basemen are in a few steps.

Leadoff hitter with good power With this guy you may start with a fastball either in a few inches or on the outside third of the plate. The other option for the first pitch is a breaking pitch just over the plate. Trust me here—*he won't swing at a breaking ball on the first pitch.* Keep mixing them up but don't give him too much credit and fall behind in the count. The pitcher is in big trouble if he falls behind in the count to a power hitter, who is almost always a great fastball hitter. A change-up will always be a great pitch to power hitters, and if the pitcher shows him hand speed he will rarely hit the ball on the sweet spot of the bat. If the pitcher has a two-run lead, the situation is completely different: pitch the power guy like the leadoff man in the first situation— *challenge him!*

Man on first, offense needs to get a runner to scoring position If you don't think the hitter is bunting (you never know for sure), then a fastball down by the knees is always a good pitch in this situation. Anytime you need a double play—and this situation certainly meets the criteria—a good fastball down in the zone is a great idea.

The coach of the offense has many options for moving the runner into scoring position: he can sacrifice bunt, steal, hit-and-run, or hit away. When the bunt is in order, which would be only in one-run games, the pitcher must know who is covering second (almost always the shortstop) if the ball is bunted hard back to him. Most teams will bunt the ball toward the first-base line because the third baseman is charging hard; the second baseman then covers first. *It is very important to get an out on this play.* Lots of teams use the fake bunt and swing, or what is called the "slash."

With a good runner on first, a steal is always a possibility, and a pitcher should be aware of the runner's lead. Every pitcher should have a quick pitch with an unloading time (the elapsed time from first movement to when the ball hits the catcher's glove) of 1.3 seconds or less. The pitcher really can't do anything about the hit-and-run except keep the runner close with pickoff moves to first, throw strikes, get ahead in the count, and stay there. If the pitcher gets two quick strikes, he limits the flexibility of the opposing manager. So throw strikes.

Runner on second base, no outs With a runner on second and nobody out, the hitter should be trying to get the runner over to third. He may either bunt the man over to third or try to hit the ball to the right side. For some right-handed hitters, the pitcher can try to keep the first two pitches in with something on them. For a pull-type hitter, these are difficult pitches to hit to right. Many other right-handed hitters who handle the bat well are fair at hitting that pitch to the right side, and the best pitch to them would be an off-speed breaking pitch or change-up. If a left-handed hitter is at the plate, it is wise to stay outside with fastballs and not throw too many off-speed pitches in this situation. One of the easiest things for a left-handed hitter to do is pull a ball to the right side and get a man over to third. Don't make it easy for the hitter and throw a lot of off-speed pitches. A team that gets an important potential run to third with one out will score most of the time.

Man on third and less than two outs When a runner reaches third with less than two outs, the defense is very vulnerable. If the runner represents the tying or winning run, the infield will probably play in and almost any hard-hit grounder will get through. Since a sacrifice fly will beat you, the pitcher must keep the ball down.

The squeeze is something that a pitcher must always be aware of whenever a runner is on third with one out. In my opinion, *a pitcher should always pitch from the stretch with a man on third and one out or any time that the infield is playing in*. Pitching from the windup here is asking for trouble, regardless of the pitch thrown or the hitter at the plate.

Pitching with a big lead I disagree with managers who say, "We're leading by 6 runs—if you give up 3 or 4, we still win. Throw the ball down the middle." Hey—if *I'm* pitching, I don't want to give up *any* runs. Sure I'm a "team guy," but I have pride, and I care about my E.R.A. Any pitcher who says he doesn't is not being honest.

First-pitch strikes, from Little League to the majors

When baseball managers, coaches, or pitching instructors get together and talk about pitching in general and what they expect from their pitchers, the subject of first-pitch strikes always comes up. *It is a fact that hitters hit for a much lower average after a first-pitch strike than after a first-pitch ball.*

Winning pitchers at all levels pitch ahead in the count, and they avoid the counts of 2-0, 3-1, and 3-2. A big step in that direction is a first-pitch strike. Generally speaking, a .300 hitter hits a hundred points higher when ahead in the count and a hundred points lower when behind in the count.

If a pitcher is concerned that so many hitters are first-pitch-fastball hitters, he shouldn't worry. The major league average on first pitches is under .200. If you are a pitcher or a pitching coach looking for an edge, consider that hitters at all levels must average near .100 against first-pitch breaking balls. *The downside to this is that most hitters absolutely hammer the pitcher who misses with a breaking-ball first pitch and as a habit comes back with a fastball down the middle on the second pitch.* At the higher levels, pitchers must stay away from fastballs down the middle on obvious fastball counts.

If the pitcher says, "I don't want to get beat on my third-best pitch," remember that on these counts the fastball *is* your third-best pitch. A pitcher who doesn't learn to throw something other than a fastball when he's behind in the count will *never* become a good pitcher.

It is also very important to get the lead-off hitter out. In the major leagues, when the leadoff hitter gets on base he scores 44 percent of the time.

Calling your own Game: When and How to Use Your Pitches

Every successful pitcher develops a variety of sequences to get hitters out. In high school, most pitchers throw fastballs until two strikes, curveballs until 3-2, and then another fastball. Not very scientific, but it works pretty well—especially if you have a good fastball.

When pitchers move into college or minor league baseball they suddenly need a change-up, and they begin the long process of developing this key pitch. This development may take some time but is a necessary ingredient, for most pitchers can't pitch in college or beyond with just two pitches.

Once a pitcher has command of at least three pitches, he can use some of the following pitch sequences. Obviously, the pitcher must adjust this information to (1) the game situation, (2) whether the hitter has power, and (3) whether the previous pitch was a strike or a ball.

Every successful pitcher pays attention to hitters' tendencies and habits. Most batters have definite hitting patterns on specific pitches and specific counts. Pitchers should also pay special attention to where their defense is playing. Communication between pitchers and catchers and other defensive players is very important to the overall success of a team. At times you even see major league pitchers pitch hitters one way when the defense is set up the other way. In my opinion, if the pitcher doesn't like the way his defense is positioned, he should move them.

The following examples of pitch sequences are for right-handed pitchers—for left-handers, simply switch the side of the plate that the hitter is swinging from.

First pitch—fastball in (right-handed hitter) Suggested pitch to follow:

- Breaking pitch away. This is the oldest and most popular sequence of all. Why? *Because it still works.*
- Another fastball in. He may think that you are going away; when you back up (repeat) a pitch it usually works well.
- Change-up. The hitter's bat has been speeded up looking for a ball to pull, and he should be out in front of the change-up.
- Cutter or slider in to the inside corner (throw at the hitter's hip). The hitter will give ground and take the pitch. Even if he gets good wood on it, it will usually go foul.

First pitch—fastball for a strike at the knees (right-handed or left-handed hitter) Suggested pitch to follow:

- Another fastball letter high. Many hitters, especially uppercutters, will chase the ball up out of the strike zone time after time. This is called "going up the ladder."
- Change-up. A change-up is always a good pitch following a fastball. Hitters will swing at a change-up anytime the pitcher

shows the hand speed—that all important ingredient—to fool the hitter.

First pitch—fastball on the outside third of the plate (right-handed hitter) Suggested pitch to follow:

- Fastball in. Once the hitter sees a pitch away, he could be diving into the pitch and the fastball in will jam him. Using the fastball in and out is one of the basic sequences for pitchers at all levels.
- Fastball away again. Remember—backing up a pitch is always a good idea, especially if you reversed the sequence (see first example) during the last at-bat.
- Change-up. Anytime you get the hitter thinking fastball, the change-up is a great pitch.
- Slider or cutter away. Hitter will chase this pitch or take it for a strike if you can get it to the outside corner.

First pitch—breaking ball on the outside half of the plate (right-handed hitter) Suggested pitch to follow:

- Fastball in. The hitter is looking away and "diving" to cover the outside half of the plate. This pitch sequence is used by pitchers at all levels.
- Another breaking ball farther away. You have the hitter diving; he may chase anything outside, even out of the strike zone.
- Fastball letter high over the plate. After a breaking-ball strike, the hitter is anxious to swing at any fastball and is likely to chase a fastball out of the strike zone.

First pitch—change-up down the middle (right-handed or left-handed hitter) Suggested pitch to follow:

- Another change if the first is a strike. Hitters usually look fastball most of the time, and backing up a change-up really works.
- High fastball. Hitters become frustrated after seeing a change for a strike and get very aggressive. High fastballs are pitches that aggressive hitters love to chase.
- Fastball in exact location of change-up (previous pitch). The closer the fastball is to the previous change-up the more

effective it is. (A straight change with the same spin as your fastball is the most effective.) Keep in mind that the change-up must show the necessary hand speed to fool the hitter.

- Fastball in. You have the hitter thinking "stay back and wait"; now you bust him in with a good fastball. It sounds very basic, and it is. It also works.

First pitch—four-seam fastball in (left-handed hitter)
Suggested pitch to follow:

- Two-seam fastball in. The fastball looks in and comes back to hit the inside corner.
- Change-up. The hitter thinks "be quick" and speeds up his bat, which makes him easy prey for the change in speeds.
- Another fastball in. The hitter might be diving in thinking you may go away after the fastball in.
- Slow curveball. The vast change in speeds from fastball to slow curveball will almost always fool the hitter and at least make him hit the ball poorly.

First pitch—four-seam fastball on the outside third of the plate (left-handed hitter) Suggested pitch to follow:

- Another four-seamer away if the first one was a strike. Every hitter you face must show you that he can hit the fastball away (many hitters can't). Until the hitter shows you the ability to adjust, keep pumping him fastballs away with an occasional one in.
- Fastball in. The hitter might be diving out for the next one and this pitch should jam him. Always remember that in-and-out sequences are almost always effective.
- Change-up away. It looks like the same pitch, and the outside change-up is by far the toughest to wait on for the hitter.
- Two-seam fastball (tailing away). The hitter may chase this one out of the strike zone if the first fastball was a four-seamer that was fairly true in flight. Taking something off this pitch (maybe four or five miles per hour) is also very effective. Professional baseball people call this practice (taking something off) a batting practice (B.P.) fastball or a "dead fish."

First pitch—breaking pitch away ("back-door") on the corner (left-handed hitter) Suggested pitch to follow:

- Another back-door breaking pitch a bit slower or farther out if the first one is a strike. You never know—he may chase it. Remember the golden rule: "Don't throw a hitter strikes if he will swing at balls."
- Fastball in. The hitter might be diving in, and the fastball in is always a good pitch here. Watch the hitter's reaction to the first pitch: did he dive in to get it or was he opening up looking for the ball inside?
- Fastball away. He probably told himself, "wait on the ball and hit it the other way." He probably won't get to the fastball and hit it on the head of the bat.
- Slider or cutter inside. If the hitter is diving, this pitch should tie him up and the result is usually a pop-up or a weak ground ball.

First pitch—slider or cutter in on the belt (left-handed hitter) Suggested pitch to follow:

- Same pitch but farther in. If he chased the first one, he may do it again. Remember to keep this pitch at least up by the belt or higher. Most left-handed hitters are dangerous when the ball is low and in.
- Two-seam fastball away. The hitter has opened up some after being crowded by the slider or cutter. Often he will "roll over" this sinker and hit a weak ground ball.
- Change-up. The change is always a good pitch after coming in on the hitter.

These are just a few examples of sequences that successful major league pitchers use. Study big-league pitchers on television or at the ballpark and try some of their sequences. Remember: *think* when you pitch—don't just throw.

DEFENSIVE PLAYS FOR THE PITCHER

During the past few years the running game in baseball has reached new levels of effectiveness. Almost without exception high school, college, and pro teams have three or more players with basestealing speed. Coaches are doing a better job teaching

2-35. When a pitcher steps off the rubber before he breaks his hands, he then becomes an infielder and cannot balk.

runners how to get better jumps, run on better counts, and pick up telltale mannerisms by pitchers that give them an advantage. Teams also are using the hit-and-run more than ever before.

Using the Stretch

With runners on base, the pitcher uses the set position (stretch). The rules require the pitcher to follow a sequence of movements to come set:

1. The pitcher must take the sign with his foot in contact with the rubber and with his hands clearly separated.
2. After getting the sign, the pitcher must bring his hands together and pause a full second before delivering the ball to home plate. While in this set position, he can move only his head. Any movements with the shoulders, legs, hands, or anything else will result in a balk. Once a pitcher starts

moving his hands it must be without interruption until he reaches the set position.

3. The pitcher may step off the rubber at any time during the sequence without balking. (The pitcher should be trained to step back off the rubber (fig. 2-35) anytime he becomes confused with signs or runners or if time is called.) He cannot split his hands until his rear foot is off the rubber.

Throwing to the Bases

A pitcher must step almost directly to any base that he chooses to throw to (the base must be occupied by a runner). He may also step and fake a throw to second or third base, but he may not fake to first base unless he steps off the rubber first. When the pitcher steps off the rubber properly, it's impossible to balk.

Right-Handers Throwing to First

Right-handed and left-handed pitchers are both required to step across a 45-degree line toward first base (fig. 2-36) when throwing to first. The right-handed pitcher can't spin the heel of his left foot while throwing to first base. Umpires will demand that he clearly

2-36. This 45-degree line is the same for left-handers and right-handers.

2-37. The right-handers must step over the line with the left foot when throwing to first.

2-38. Left-handers must step over the line with the right foot when throwing to first.

step over the line (fig. 2-37 and fig. 2-38). All pitchers should have the ability to throw to first in the middle of the stretch and prior to becoming set. The goal should be to get the ball to the first baseman within one second of the first movement (major league pitchers get the ball to first in .85 to 1.00 seconds). Holding the ball in the set position for different periods of time before delivery is very effective against would-be basestealers.

Left-Handers Throwing to First

Some left-handers are able to freeze runners by pausing when the right knee gets to its highest point. They then try to read the runner. If the runner has been held until this point, the left-hander has in fact prevented most steals. Runners will try to see mechanical differences in the deliveries to home and first. When they can't pick up any differences, they usually take a smaller lead and then break on the pitcher's first movement. Many runners use this method, so it's important that left-handers work on a fast delivery to the plate. Left-handers should develop at least two alternatives to the conventional move. One obvious alternative is using different tempos for the regular move.

Setup move This is the conventional move with the pitcher bringing his right leg up and down with the same tempo and throwing to first base. The pitcher should "show" the setup move and follow it with the pickoff move.

Pickoff move The same move but at a different tempo. The pitcher brings his right leg up with the same tempo as the setup move but then drives the foot down (across the line) at twice the speed and throws the ball to first base with a snap throw. This move is a must to help prevent runners from going on the pitcher's first movement.

Step-back move A step-back move is a must for left-handers. Once the pitcher becomes set, he steps back off the rubber with his left foot and in almost one motion throws to first with a snap throw (fig. 2-39); however, he must remember to step off the

2-39. The step-back move is used by many left-handers. The pitcher steps back with his left foot and then splits his hands and makes a snap throw to first.

rubber *before* breaking his hands. This move is very effective against a runner who tries to get one more step as the stretch sequence begins or leans toward second just before he breaks.

Unloading Time

All pitchers should work on their unloading time—the elapsed time from the pitcher's first movement until the ball hits the catcher's glove when pitching out of the stretch. Major league pitchers unload the ball in 1.0 to 1.7 seconds, although those with times slower than 1.3 are generally easy to steal on. So pitchers at the higher levels of baseball must strive to develop a delivery time of 1.2 to 1.3 seconds. Trying to decrease this unloading time too quickly can destroy natural mechanics, so this must be a gradual process over a period of 60–90 days. The natural movements should not be altered but be performed at a slightly faster rate.

The Pickoff at Second Base

Many variations of the pickoff play are used at second base, but the most common and also the most effective is called the "daylight play." It is designed to work with no sign and can be used at the infielders' discretion. The shortstop moves in behind the runner (just off his inside shoulder) as the pitcher is becoming set. If the runner moves back a step or two, then the shortstop goes back to his position and the pitcher delivers the ball to the plate. But if the runner moves off or stands his ground, the shortstop breaks toward the bag and shows the pitcher the open glove (fig. 2-40). When the pitcher sees this "daylight" between the runner and the bag he turns and throws for the pickoff. The second baseman can also run the play using the open hand—the real difference is that he doesn't have the runner in front of him (fig. 2-41). A good variation of the play is to have the shortstop come in behind the runner, return to his position, and then have the second baseman break as the shortstop retreats (many times the third base coach will tell the runner "you're all right" when he sees the shortstop retreating, and the runner will take an extra step). Some teams use a variety of timing plays at second base. For the most part, they take too much time in practice and seldom work enough to help you win games. In my opinion, the daylight play is the only pickoff needed at second base.

2-40. On the "daylight" pickoff play at second, the shortstop shows the open glove and the pitcher turns and throws.

2-41. The second baseman runs the same play and gives the open hand.

2-42. With runners on first and second, as the left-handed pitcher lifts his leg the first baseman breaks for the bag to take the pickoff throw.

2-43. The right-handed pitcher looks to second, sees the first baseman break for the bag, and then turns to make the pickoff throw.

Pickoff with Runners on First and Second Base

Since the first baseman plays behind the runner on this play, a sign is necessary to avoid miscommunication. Most clubs use a "pick and rub" sign: the person initiating the play (first baseman or pitcher) "picks" at his uniform and the other player "rubs" to acknowledge the sign.

With a left-handed pitcher, the first baseman breaks when the pitcher lifts his right leg (fig. 2-42). A right-hander executing the play comes set and looks to second so he can see the first baseman in his peripheral vision (fig. 2-43). When the first baseman breaks, he turns and throws to first base. This play does require some practice but works well with good timing and a good throw.

Pickoffs at Third Base

For a right-handed pitcher the pickoff at third base is basically the same as the pickoff at first for a left-hander; conversely, a left-handed pitcher works the play just as a right-hander does at first. However, pickoffs at third often cause as many problems as they solve. The play requires good timing and will eat up valuable practice time. For most coaches it is simply not worth it. The pitcher is allowed to fake to third anytime he wishes—this will usually hold the runner close enough without the risk of a balk or a throwing error.

Working from a Windup or Stretch

It is a good idea to pitch from a stretch with a man on third and one out—you will rarely see a squeeze with no outs and never with two outs. It also is advisable to pitch from the stretch anytime the infield is playing in. The runner can obviously get a better jump when the pitcher is in a windup, and a step or two means a great deal at home plate on a close play.

When the pitcher uses the windup with a runner on third, runners on second and third, or the bases loaded, the key element is balance. In order to step back off the rubber without balking, he must step back with his pivot foot (right foot for a right-handed pitcher). If he should step back with his free foot, he would be using the same initial movement that starts the windup and would therefore deceive the runner, and a balk would be called. The pitcher can step off with the proper foot much easier if his weight is equally distributed.

When the Squeeze Is in Order

Whenever there is a runner on third with one out, you must assume a squeeze is a possibility (depending on the score). The runner on third should break when the pitcher's stride foot hits. If he breaks early, or the hitter gives away the squeeze early, the pitcher should pitch out with the pitch that is called. Some ball clubs believe that the pitcher should knock down a right-handed batter in this situation. A pitchout works better and is less dangerous; besides, the hitter can still bunt a pitch up and in and beat you.

Fielding

Every pitcher must understand the importance of being a good fielder. (However, pitchers should never alter their deliveries to finish in a better fielding position—fielding may be important, but getting the most out of your pitches is your top priority.) By following a few basic mechanical fundamentals, a pitcher can easily make fielding part of his overall development. First, bend with the legs and not with the back (see Chapter 3). Second, line up your feet toward the target (fig. 2-44). It is a good idea to keep the ball out in front of your body at all times (fig. 2-45)—never let the ball get under your body or between your legs (fig. 2-46). Finally, a smooth weight transfer, or "crow hop," will add to the smoothness and overall rhythm of your throw.

Covering first base The pitcher should break toward first base on every ball hit to the first-base side of the diamond. He must head for a spot approximately six feet from the bag on the baseline and make one cut up the line (fig. 2-47) so that he is running parallel to the baseline (fig. 2-48). It is very important that he shorten his strides as he approaches the bag in the event of a bad throw. It may be necessary to stop at the bag and receive the throw as a first baseman would. The pitcher should touch the inside third of the bag (fig. 2-49) with the right foot only, so that he can push off into fair territory and avoid the runner. This way,

2-44. Always line up the feet toward the target.

2-45. Field the ball in front of the body at all times.

2-46. Never allow the ball to get under the body or between the legs.

2-47. On every ball hit to the first-base side, the pitcher should break toward first, heading for a spot about six feet from the baseline.

2-48. The pitcher should then make one cut up the line so that he is running parallel to the baseline.

2-49. The pitcher should touch the inside part of the bag with the right foot only, so that he can push off into fair territory and avoid the runner.

his momentum should never carry him into foul territory or into the path of the runner.

The pitcher will also have to cover first on the first baseman-to-shortstop-to-pitcher double play. He will need to get to the base, turn to face second, and receive the throw as a first baseman would. It is a good idea to give the person fielding the ball a good target with two hands whenever possible.

Bunts and comebackers with nobody on base With nobody on, the pitcher usually has lots of time to make most fielding plays. Many mistakes are caused by the pitcher rushing the play or failing to get his feet into proper alignment. The old cliché "step in the direction of your throw" is good advice—many throwing errors happen because of poor direction.

After receiving the ball (with two hands if possible), the pitcher should follow his glove—right-handers turn counterclockwise, left-handers turn clockwise—when turning toward his target. There will be some bunts toward the lines or with a very fast

2-50. In some situations there will be no time for a crow hop—the pitcher will have to simply plant his back leg and throw.

runner when the pitcher must simply plant his back foot (right foot for right-handers) and throw with no time for a crow hop (fig. 2-50).

Bunt plays and comebackers with runners on base The pitcher must know the game situation at all times. Before the play starts, he must know which middle infielder is covering second and what bunt plays (if any) are on. Basically, all bunt plays are designed to get an out at a certain base, and coaches will be better off sticking to simple bunt defenses. With a runner on first only, runners on first and second, or runners on first and third with less than two outs, a double play started by the pitcher is a possibility. When the ball is hit back toward a pitcher he should catch the ball with two hands if possible, listen for the catcher to tell him which base to throw to, follow his glove direction, and step in the direction of the base that he is throwing to. A throw chest high over the bag thrown at 80 percent velocity will produce the best results.

Backing up the bases After the pitcher delivers the ball to the plate, he becomes an infielder. He not only has fielding responsibilities but must direct traffic and help teammates on pop-ups and back up bases (see defensive responsibilities in Chapter 8).

A pitcher has a place to go every time the ball is hit, and many games are won by pitchers who back up the proper base using the proper method. He should read the throw from the outfield and get as deep as possible behind the base. Many times a pitcher will stand on the mound feeling sorry for himself when a ball is hit in the gap, get over too late to back up the play, and then feel worse as the overthrow ends up in the dugout and more runners score. Pitchers should study the playbook and know their responsibilities on every defensive play.

COACHES' CORNER: SOLVING PITCHING PROBLEMS

If you are a coach and you have turned directly to this page seeking quick solutions to the problems you face, this section won't help you. You will not be able to communicate with your pitchers about their deliveries until you have given your pitchers a basic program of mechanics and fundamentals. Your pitchers don't need to be experts, but they need to understand how important balance and direction are to their overall success. They must know what rushing is and how it affects their delivery. They must understand what the balance point is and how it relates to consistency. *Once the pitchers understand these fundamentals, and only then, can you correct their mechanics.* So take a few minutes to read the mechanics section of this chapter.

A pitching coach should be able to

- trace a problem to its root (many people just work on the symptoms)
- research the problem and come up with a plan of attack
- give the pitcher information that will help him immediately as well as in the long run (if you do not offer some kind of short-term help, he will lose confidence in you)

All pitchers' mechanical problems fall into one of three categories:

1. *Direction.* Moving the head off center at any time during the delivery will result in a loss of balance. A pitcher should keep his head dead still until he reaches the balance point and then move his head directly forward and down toward the target until the ball is released.

2. *Rushing*. A pitcher will rush his delivery if he doesn't stay back over his back foot until he reaches the balance point or if his stride is too quick.

3. *Extension*. To deliver the ball effectively, the pitcher should extend out over his front knee (left knee for a right-handed pitcher) as he releases the ball. This movement not only protects the arm against injury but helps promote solid direction with the head.

The balance drill Working from the mound, the pitcher makes 20–30 throws to a coach positioned about two-thirds of the distance between the rubber and home plate (40–50 feet). The pitches should be half-speed fastballs, and the pitcher should work from both a windup and a stretch.

The emphasis in this drill should be on direction and controlling the ball laterally with the head: the front shoulder leads, the head stays on line, and after delivery the pitcher lines up his *back* shoulder with the desired direction of the flight of the ball. The balance drill also helps the pitcher keep his head down and finish his delivery, which in turn helps in getting his backside through and completing the weight transfer.

Controlling the ball vertically is a process of timing and tempo, but every pitcher at every age and skill level can be taught to control the ball laterally using this "front shoulder, head, back shoulder" method. As a major league pitching coach, I use this drill *every day* with nearly all of my pitchers.

Problems and Solutions

Pitching coaches should remember that most pitchers are wild when they are young. Unless a pattern develops, you shouldn't jump in and start changing mechanics too quickly. Be patient and some problems will work themselves out with a little positive talk and a few hundred innings.

(Note: In the following troubleshooting section, directional references assume the perspective of a pitcher looking toward home plate. Also, in discussions of mechanics, examples and ideas are expressed in terms of right-handed pitchers.)

Problem 1

"My pitcher has no command with any of his pitches."

Solution

Always look to the mental first—you don't want to get into the mechanics if you don't have to.

He could be giving the hitters too much credit and just throwing for the corners—trying to "miss bats"—instead of being aggressive in the strike zone. Tell him to believe in his stuff and challenge the hitters. Ask him to tell you what he is seeing when he looks at the catcher. He should be centering on the glove and should not see the hitter or the whole catcher. Remember—the pitcher should not watch the flight of the ball but instead zero in on the catcher's glove.

The next step is to address the balance and direction issues. Is he keeping his head still until he gets to the balance point? If the answer is no, then slow him down. If the answer is yes, then he may be okay at the balance point and then take his head off line by leaning back or drifting off center as he strides. If he has balance problems, then you can bet that he is trying to overthrow, and slowing him down can't hurt. When a pitcher overthrows, the front shoulder and hips open before the stride foot lands. If he is opening up, then you must have him throw half-speed from 50 feet or so for a couple of workouts and counsel him on the importance of keeping the front shoulder closed and going directly at the catcher. Be patient—pitchers who are wild are more frustrated than anyone by the walks and the wild pitches. A good pitching coach will avoid making comments like "just throw strikes" or "let them hit it"—these suggestions won't help at all. A little positive reinforcement goes a long way in this case.

Problem 2

"My pitcher has started throwing his curveball high."

Solution

Many times just slowing the speed of the curve may help.

If throwing the curveball easier doesn't work, the pitcher is probably leaning off to the first-base side while on his way to the plate. Many pitchers do this to try to get farther on top of their curveballs. They want them to break straight down, and this is simply not necessary—many major leaguers have great three-quarter curves. A pitcher should throw his curve from the same arm slot as he does his fastball.

Problem 3
"My pitcher has started throwing all of his curves in the dirt."

Solution
Almost without exception, extension is the problem.

When a pitcher throws his curveball consistently in the dirt, he is probably "biting it off." By that I mean that he is not extending forward and releasing the ball far enough in front. Have the catcher stand up and make the pitcher throw him several curves chest high. He must get the concept of throwing his curve out in front and letting it break. The curve is supposed to be an off-speed pitch, and the pitcher who tries to muscle it will never master a consistent spin.

Problem 4
"One of my pitchers always misses inside and outside."

Solution
The solution here always centers around good direction.

The head controls the flight of the ball horizontally. Even if the front side is flying open, or if another mechanical problem prohibits good balance, keeping the head still will almost always help. Most pitchers who miss consistently in and out do so because they don't control the movement of the head.

Have the catcher stand up and move three feet to the left of home plate. Instruct the pitcher to wind up and take his entire front side toward the catcher, paying special attention to aiming the head *directly* toward the mitt. After a few throws, have the catcher move three feet to the right of the plate. By working from side to side, the pitcher will learn the value of leading with the head and will gain the skill to use his head to control the ball laterally. Also stress that not only should the front shoulder and head go straight at the target but *the back shoulder should also finish in a direct line to the target.* Use this drill as often as necessary to reestablish this concept. *In addition, this pitcher needs the balance drill daily.*

Problem 5

"My pitcher is missing up and down."

Solution

When a pitcher misses vertically it is a more complicated problem.

The first area to address is the back leg (right leg for a right-handed pitcher). The leg should be in a strong position to support the foundation of the delivery. If the leg breaks down too much, the pitcher will end up throwing "uphill," and the resulting pitch almost always will be high. This symptom will show up when the pitcher's shoulders are tilted back at a considerable angle at the balance point. Many times "casting," or throwing the left leg out instead of lifting it in a controlled manner, will cause this. If the shoulders are tilted and this appears to be the root of the problem, then make the pitcher stand erect as he makes his turn and gets to his balance position. Make him keep his shoulders level and maintain this position until he starts forward to the plate. He must understand the concept of feeling like he is throwing "downhill" in order to have proper leverage. This should bring the ball down into the strike zone.

Another reason why pitchers throw the ball high is rushing, a problem that every pitcher faces throughout his career. When the front side opens too soon or the stride is too quick, the arm arc is cut down (it doesn't have time to make the full circle) and the result is a lower release of the ball (the hand starts forward from a lower position). The pitcher pushes the ball uphill, and it goes high. In order to attack this problem, you must slow down the stride and/or front side. The front side must be thought of as directional only. *If a pitcher uses the front side as a powerful movement, rushing is inevitable.* Slow down the delivery and the rush will be controlled.

When the pitcher is constantly throwing the ball low, most of the time extension is the problem—refer to problem 3. Another reason for missing low is overcompensation after throwing a high pitch: everyone is telling the pitcher to throw the ball lower, so he does.

Problem 6

"My pitcher has no confidence in and no command of his change-up."

Solution

Wait a minute! Have you given the change-up enough time to develop?

If you are sure that you have given the pitcher at least enough time to develop a change-up to a reasonable level, then here are a few solutions to consider:

Most problems associated with the change-up are centered around the arm speed and the thought process involved. The pitcher seems to worry too much about whether the change-up is too fast. Consequently, he tries to slow down the ball with his arm. *But the grip must do 100 percent of the job of slowing the ball down*—this can't be stressed too much. Whenever a pitcher slows the ball down with his arm, he is no longer showing the hitter the hand speed necessary to fool him.

The grip usually is not the culprit unless the pitcher has been struggling with the same grip for quite some time. If the concept of a straight change-up is just not working, the coach and pitcher should consider a change to the split as a change-up (see "Changing Speeds").

Direction is also critical to throwing the change-up. If the head comes off line even the slightest bit, it destroys the consistency of the change-up. The head must stay straight on line and come down to the glove until the ball has been released.

3
PLAYING THE INFIELD

USING THE RIGHT GLOVE

Most young infielders use gloves that are too big for them. A glove
is not a piece of equipment that you can grow into. Shortstops and
second basemen should use a glove that is small, light, and flexible
(fig. 3-1); third basemen can use a slightly bigger glove; and, of
course, first basemen should wear the trapper's glove. A middle
infielder can lose the ball in a glove that is too big; the sheer
weight of such a glove will be too much for young players to
handle. The infielder not only will have trouble with the exchange
but also may develop bad fielding habits that will last a lifetime.

THROWING WITH STRENGTH AND ACCURACY

Whenever possible, infielders should hold the ball across the seams
when throwing. By playing catch they can learn to find the seams
quite easily; after a while they will automatically throw across the
seams. Even if they don't always attain the perfect grip, they will
notice gradual improvement.

    As they prepare to throw, infielders must "close off" the front
side (fig. 3-2) for maximum leverage. All players should try to

3-1. The shortstop and second baseman should use a smaller glove than other players in order to handle the ball better.

throw overhand (or at least three-quarters); however, there are lots of plays that require an underhand snap throw. They should watch the target, not the ball in flight. Just as dart players watch the bull's-eye, they must not only watch the target but step toward it and transfer their weight in that direction. Throwing accuracy and arm strength are a combination of athletic ability, concentration, mechanics, and practice.

Players who have trouble with accuracy on their throws (almost every young infielder) don't have a program. When throwing across the infield or throwing to a base as a relay man on balls

3-2. The infielder should close off the front side of the body in order to throw properly.

coming from the outfield, infielders should see a very small target. Ask players what they see as they throw on a routine play to first and most will tell you "the first baseman." That's okay, but infielders get better results over the long haul when they fine center on a specific target, such as the first baseman's letters or his cap.

THE GAME SITUATION AND POSITIONING

An infielder must be aware of the game situation: He should check the baserunners and think about what their runs represent. He should watch the opposing coaches and the hitter in case they tip their offensive plans. He should watch his coach, his pitcher, and his catcher in case someone is putting on a pickoff play. Obviously, he should know the number of outs and the speed of the hitter and runners on base. Being aware of the game situations and mentally rehearsing the play will greatly increase the infielder's defensive effectiveness. Players who rehearse the possible plays will react properly when the ball is actually hit to them.

Depending on the game situation and the tendencies of the hitter, infielders will position themselves at different depths and different angles from the hitter. It is very important that the infielders know and look at the catcher's signs. They must know what pitch is coming so that they may anticipate which direction the ball will tend to be hit. Infielders must remember not to move early because the hitter will see movement and know what pitch is coming. I have seen major league infielders give away pitches without realizing it. The pitcher gets bombed, the team loses, and no one can figure out what happened. One young National League second baseman gives away almost every pitch: every time an off-speed pitch is coming to a right-handed hitter he takes a step toward the middle; when a left-hander is up, he takes a step to pull (toward first base); and if a fastball is coming, he doesn't move at all. The Houston Astros hit the ball very well when he is playing second base against us.

The regular position—"straight away"—for the middle infielders is about halfway between the bases in line with the mound. The depth depends on the infielder's throwing arm strength and the speed of the runner at the plate: For the third baseman it is usually four or five steps off the line and two or three steps behind the baseline (again depending on arm strength, speed of the runner, and also if he is likely to bunt). The first baseman should play as deep as possible while still being able to get to the bag to set up for the throw. Some first basemen, notably Will Clark and Mark Grace, play very deep and have lots of range and are still able to hustle and get to the bag in time. The first baseman should also play four or five steps off the line, unless a left-handed pull hitter is up; in that case, three steps is the proper distance from the line. In my opinion, most first basemen in the majors play too close to the line and not nearly deep enough.

When the double play is in order, the middle infielders must cheat over to double-play depth. This position is generally two steps in and two steps over from the regular position. The third baseman must also take a couple of steps in to cut down the overall elapsed time of the potential double play (the average runner in the majors goes down the line to first in 4.4 seconds). If the first baseman is holding the runner on first, he must "bounce" off with the delivery of the ball home to cover more ground. If he is behind a runner on first (with runners on first and second or bases loaded), he must be close enough to make the double play work.

When the coach or manager wants the infield in, he is referring to a position just inside the baseline. From this position, the infielder should be able to get the runner at the plate on a routine ground ball. With a slow runner on third, the infielder can back off a step or two from the baseline. He shouldn't be concerned with other runners, as they must avoid a fielder who is in the process of fielding a ball in play. The infielders should remind the pitcher that he should pitch from the stretch position any time that the infield is playing in to cut off the run.

Some coaches position their infielders "halfway." It has always been my opinion that these guys just can't make a decision. When the infield is halfway between regular depth and in, they can't make either play: they are too deep to get the runner at the plate and are too shallow to have any range and stop a big inning from developing. The coach must decide if he wants to give up the run or cut it down at the plate. It takes a little courage, but a decision must be made and the team has to live with the consequences. Coaching is not an exact science.

3-3. The starting position, while the pitcher is getting his signs and before the ball is delivered.

FIELDING MECHANICS FOR INFIELDERS

The Starting Position

The starting position refers to a relaxed position in which the infielder is anticipating that the ball will be hit to him. The hands can be on the knees or hanging relaxed at the side. The feet are just a little bit more than shoulder-width apart and the legs bent slightly (fig. 3-3). By the time the infielder assumes this starting position, he has already done all of his homework (number of outs, game situation, etc.). He has already rehearsed the play to anticipate what he will do if the ball is hit to him on the ground hard, on the ground softly, to his right, to his left, or lined at him.

The Ready Position

When the pitcher begins his windup or delivers the ball to the plate from the stretch, the infielder should switch from the starting position to the ready position (fig. 3-4). This position is similar to

3-4. The ready position, with the legs flexed and the hands low and relaxed—this infielder is ready to move in any direction.

that of a basketball player or a football defensive back guarding another player. He should be relaxed but ready to break in any direction. The weight is forward on the balls of the feet and not back on the heels.

As the ball approaches home plate and the hitting area, the infielder should take two small steps forward in order to put his body in motion. This allows for a quicker start—it overcomes the inertia, or dead weight, of the body. It is not a good idea to start from a dead stop. All major league infielders and most outfielders make this little two-step movement (with some players it may look more like a little jump) as the ball reaches the hitter.

Fielding Ground Balls

Infielders moving either to the right or the left to field ground balls should use a crossover step: the first step should be with the away leg instead of the leg nearest the ball. When a ball is hit to the right, the player should pivot on his right foot and cross over with his left leg (fig. 3-5); on balls hit to the left, he should pivot on his left foot and cross over with his right leg (fig. 3-6). The infielder should make every effort to get in front of and control the ball.

When the infielder has to extend to his left to get the ball (fig. 3-7), he must get his feet underneath him as quickly as possible for balance. After gaining balance, he must plant the right foot before he can make his throw (fig. 3-8). During this process, he must close off his upper body to get something on the throw.

3-5. The crossover left step is used to go to the right.

3-6. When going to the left, the infielder uses the crossover right step.

3-7. When the infielder extends to the left, body balance is very important.

3-8. The infielder must collect himself and get his feet underneath him in preparation for the throw.

On balls hit to his right that he cannot get in front of, he will have to backhand the ball, and at times he will be going away from the throwing target. He should try to field the ball with his left foot down (fig. 3-9), plant the right foot while closing off the hips and shoulders (fig. 3-10), and push off to throw while transferring the weight back to the left foot (fig. 3-11).

3-9. When the ball is hit to his right, the infielder should field the ball with his left foot down, if possible.

3-10. Closing off the front side is an important part of making the play in the hole.

3-11. It is important to throw the ball overhand when making a long throw across the infield.

When the infielder approaches the ball he should slow down, get under control, and bend with the legs (fig. 3-12) and not bend the back (fig. 3-13). Fielders who bend over with stiff legs have poor balance and cannot react to the ball if it takes a bad hop. When he lowers his glove to receive the ball, he must open the glove—the glove will not open by itself. When the player tries to

3-12. An infielder must bend with the legs when going down after a ground ball.

3-13. Infielders with stiff legs cannot react to balls that take bad hops; in addition, they take more time to recover and make the throw.

receive the ball with the glove halfway open (fig. 3-14), he must be perfect. If he makes the effort to practice opening the glove (fig. 3-15), he will be able to handle balls cleanly that otherwise might have hit off the side of his glove. This sounds so basic that some coaches at the higher levels take it for granted, but watch skilled infielders and you will see that even some of them go after balls with the glove half-open.

3-14. Some young players try to field ground balls with the glove halfway open. A surprising number of players at all levels make this fundamental mistake.

3-15. The infielder must remember to open the glove completely when fielding grounders.

Fielding slow-hit balls presents a special problem because the infielder must charge through the ball and throw without setting himself. Whenever possible, he should field the ball with both hands in front of the body and the left foot on the ground (fig. 3-16), transfer the ball to the throwing hand while planting the right foot and closing off the front side (fig. 3-17), and then throw the ball (fig. 3-18). This is a play that infielders seldom work on regularly and consequently do not execute well. It is difficult to work on fielding slow-hit balls during batting practice because of the danger involved, so players must practice this play either before or after batting practice.

3-16. The infielders should field slow-hit balls with the left foot on the ground and with the hands in front of the body.

3-17. He should close off his front side while picking up the target with his eyes, . . .

3-18. . . . then flip the ball in an under-hand motion.

Diving for Balls

All players should dive for balls. This skill can come in handy in a number of game situations. For example, when a runner on second represents an important run, all infielders must be prepared to dive to keep the ball in the infield. And when the infield is playing in to cut off the run, diving for the ball and simply knocking it down—without even making a play—may freeze the runner on third.

As a coach and a manager, I've noticed that only some players are willing to dive to make plays. This skill can be taught even at age six or seven with great success. At the San Diego School of Baseball players learn at that age to dive with the glove

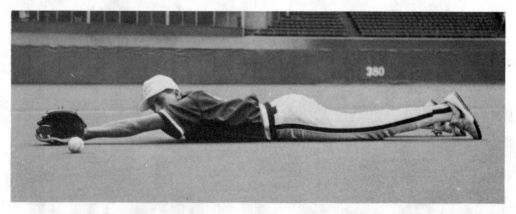

3-19. When diving for balls, players must keep the glove open when they land. This requires lots of practice.

3-20. Most players hit their elbow when they dive, which causes their glove to close; even though they get to the ball, they cannot catch it.

open (fig. 3-19), push off to get to their feet, and pick up the target for an accurate throw. It is important that they don't hit on their glove-hand elbow when they dive (fig. 3-20). Full extension of the body is also crucial: players who lay down in pieces, one body part at a time, get dirty but never reach the ball and make the play.

Tagging and Covering on Steals

With a runner on first base, the possibility of a steal or a hit-and-run play always exists. Coverage is usually dictated by which side of the plate the hitter hits from. With a left-handed hitter, the shortstop will almost always cover second; with a right-handed hitter, the second baseman has the coverage. In the major leagues, these assignments are sometimes switched from hitter to hitter or even from pitch to pitch. The shortstop will signal the second baseman (most often with an open or closed mouth) on each pitch to indicate who is covering. The switches are put on so an experienced hitter can't hit the ball through the vacated position on a hit-and-run. As the count on the hitter changes, many times the infield coverage on the steal changes. The shortstop, for instance, may see the catcher put down the sign for a slow curveball with a right-handed hitter at the plate. Since the chances are this ball will be pulled, he may signal the second baseman to cover on the steal. The infielder that is covering should take two steps toward home plate first and then break for the bag. If the player breaks directly for the bag when the basestealer breaks, he will be leaving his position too soon, making the defense very vulnerable.

When runners are on first and second, the team should have a sign for where the ball will be thrown on a double steal—you don't want more than one infielder breaking to cover a base at the same time. If the runner on first is slow, many times the throw to second instead of third will produce an easy out. It is also possible that the hitter may dictate the coverage; that is, in the case of a right-handed pull hitter, you may want the third baseman deeper and staying home (remaining in position) in case the runners are running.

On an attempted steal, the infielder has two positions to choose from: in front of the bag (fig. 3-21) or straddling the bag (fig. 3-22). When the throw arrives, he should place his glove in

3-21. Most major league infielders set up in front of the bag to make a tag.

3-22. The straddle method is also used by some big leaguers.

3-23. He should put the glove down in front of the bag and let the runner slide into it, tagging himself.

3-24. If the infielder attempts the tag with the glove open, he risks having the ball kicked loose or being cut by the spikes of the advancing baserunner.

front of the bag with the back of the hand facing the runner (fig. 3-23) in order to avoid injury. (If he doesn't protect the ball (fig. 3-24), it can be easily knocked out of the glove.) When the infielder feels the contact from the runner, he should pull the glove away. *Tagging is one thing in baseball that should be done with one hand.*

When the offensive team attempts a double steal with runners on first and third, the defense must have a set of signs or, at the very least, communicate well on the play. One option is simply to throw the ball to second and, with vocal help from the third baseman, the middle infielders will react to the runners and execute accordingly. If the runner on third does not break for the plate, the middle infielder simply tags out the baserunner from first. If the runner stops, then a rundown begins, and the other infielders must help the player with the ball if the runner on third breaks for home after the rundown starts.

Another option is called the "crash" play and is run off a sign from the catcher, who comes up and throws the ball to a middle infielder breaking straight for the plate. If the runner on third breaks on this play, he should be out.

The final three options provide for the ball being thrown directly to third, back to the pitcher, or not thrown at all. I don't recommend the use of any of these plays at the higher levels. A good defensive team should be able to throw the ball through to second and not allow the offensive team to score from third. (Note: the catcher must check the runner at third when he comes up to throw to second or the runner at third can get too large a jump and score easily.)

Going Back on Pop-Ups

When the ball is popped up over the infield, the infielders should keep going back for the ball until they hear the outfielder call for the ball (see Chapter 8 for infielders' areas of responsibilities). The infielder must be very aggressive going back on the ball and, although a collision is possible, must count on the outfielder to call loudly for the ball early enough for him to get out of his way. This can be a potentially dangerous play if the players don't communicate properly. A few years ago in the minor leagues, a shortstop died as a result of a collision with a leftfielder.

Coaches should spend lots of time hitting balls over the infielders' heads with the outfielders coming in. This will not only win ball games but will train the players to communicate better. It is wise to use a pitching machine to train the players, as most coaches are not good enough with the fungo bat to hit pop-ups that will be effective in training the infielders and outfielders.

Refer to Chapter 5 ("Playing the Sun") for suggestions on catching balls in the sun.

The Rundown Play

When a runner is caught between bases, nobody on the field should be standing and watching. Every defensive player is either directly involved in the rundown or backing up the bases or the throws.

The player with the ball who starts the rundown is called the

3-25. In a rundown, the charger holds the ball up and the receiver gives him a target.

charger—his job is to get the ball into the throwing position and run toward the baserunner, forcing him to run full speed and making him commit directionally. The person waiting for the throw is called the receiver—his job is first to align himself on the same side of the baseline as the charger; then, when the runner is 15 to 20 feet from him, he should take a step forward and say "Now" with his hands in a receiving position (fig. 3-25). The charger then throws the ball chest high, and the receiver should be able to tag the runner. The rundown will then be over in one throw. It is not a good idea for the charger to fake throws, for this has a tendency to fake out the receiver as well as the runner. If the first throw doesn't get the runner out, the backup people enter the play and the charger continues on to become a backup person (see The Playbook for rundown assignments).

Team Bunt Defenses

There are two standard bunting situations that develop on a regular basis: a runner on first with less than two outs and runners on first and second with nobody out.

With a man on first and less than two outs, the first baseman charges and the pitcher—who has held the runner at first—delivers the ball to the plate. The third baseman charges as soon as the hitter squares around to bunt. The shortstop covers second base, and the second baseman covers first. The pitcher covers the ground straight ahead toward the plate. The bunter should try to bunt the ball to the first-base side since the first baseman is the last defensive player to break. The main objective here is to get an out—somewhere. If the ball is bunted very hard right at someone, it may even be possible to go to second to begin the double play.

If there are runners on first and second with nobody out, there are three variations on the play. The first bunt play starts with the shortstop holding the runner on second and then simply covering second. The second baseman covers first, the first baseman charges aggressively, the third baseman covers third, and the pitcher covers the third-base line. If the pitcher can't field the ball, the third baseman must read the ball, go get it, and get the out at first. This play is usually called regular coverage and is used in the majority of cases.

3-26. On the wheel play, the shortstop breaks for third. When the pitcher sees daylight between the shortstop and the runner he delivers the ball to the plate.

The second variation, called the wheel play, starts the same way, but the shortstop breaks and covers third as the third baseman charges very aggressively. The second baseman still covers first and the first baseman still charges and covers the right side of the infield. The pitcher on this play first must let the shortstop break a couple steps toward third with definite daylight between him and the runner (fig. 3-26). He then delivers the ball to the plate and charges straight ahead. If daylight is not present between the shortstop and the runner, the pitcher must step off the rubber and kill the play. The object of this play is to get the runner forced at third. It should be used with a slow runner at second and the game on the line. Note that the defense is very vulnerable with everyone moving, and the coach must be reasonably sure that the hitter at the plate is going to bunt before he puts on this play.

The third variation of this play begins as the wheel play; the difference is that the ball is not delivered to the plate. When the daylight is present between the shortstop and runner, the shortstop breaks for third as he does on the wheel play. The second baseman, instead of breaking to cover first, breaks to second base for a pickoff attempt. If the runner at second takes the fake and thinks that it is a wheel play, he has a great chance of being picked off. This pickoff play would normally be used following a wheel play when the ball has been bunted foul or the pitcher has thrown a ball. Please refer to Chapter 8 for further explanation of team bunt coverage.

PLAYING SECOND BASE

Turning Double Plays

In possible double-play situations, the second baseman must cheat over to double-play depth; in other words, he should shift two steps in and two steps over toward the bag from his normal position.

There are six ways for the second baseman to start the double play:

1. When the ball is hit near the bag, the second baseman should step on the bag with the right foot (fig. 3-27) and throw to first.
2. When the ball is hit to his right but too far from the bag to take it himself, he should use the underhand toss to the shortstop (fig. 3-28) and follow through toward the bag with his body.
3. When the ball is hit right at him, he may use the backhand toss (fig. 3-29), especially useful on slow-hit balls or with a fast runner at the plate. This toss takes time to master and should only be used by advanced players.
4. When the ball is hit right at him or to his left so that he can get in front of it, he may also use the pivot. He must stay low and not take any steps but simply pivot on the balls of the feet (fig. 3-30 and fig. 3-31).
5. When the ball is hit to his left and he has to extend for it, he should use the back-door pivot (fig. 3-32 and fig. 3-33). The important movement here is to plant the right foot before throwing. This ball must be hit hard or it is best to abort the double play and get the out at first.
6. On slow-hit balls toward second, the second baseman must decide whether to try for the force at second or take the out

3-27. When the ball is hit near the bag, the second baseman should take it himself.

3-28. If he can't get to the bag himself but fields the ball near the bag, he should use the underhand toss.

3-29. The backhand toss is the fastest of all the methods used by second basemen to start the double play.

3-30 and 3-31. On grounders hit directly at the second baseman or grounders that he can get in front of, he should pivot on the balls of his feet, close off his body, and flip the ball from the side.

3-32 and 3-33. Using the back-door pivot, the infielder extends for the ball, plants the right foot, and throws after turning counterclockwise.

3-34. As the middle man on the double play, the second baseman first
pauses behind the bag at second with
his left foot on the base.

3-35. He then comes across the bag
to catch the ball, . . .

at first. The backhand flip (see fig. 3-29) must be used on
this play. Occasionally, he will have the opportunity to tag
the runner coming from first base. Baserunners will be told
to stop to avoid the tag but won't always recognize the play
developing and will run into the tag anyway.

When the second baseman is the middle man in the double
play, he must get to the bag quickly. He should delay behind the
bag with his left foot on it (fig. 3-34) until he sees the ball in flight
from the shortstop or the third baseman. He should then step
across the bag with his right foot as he receives the ball (fig. 3-35),
plant his right foot, and throw to first (fig. 3-36). Note that his left
toe is opened straight toward first: If the foot isn't opened fully
(fig. 3-37) and the leg is hit by the sliding runner, severe knee

3-36. . . . shifts his weight to his right foot, and throws to first (note that the toes are open toward the runner).

3-37. When the toes of the left foot are closed, serious knee injury can result when the runner slides into the left leg.

damage can result. The runner's job is to disrupt the double play by taking out the middle infielder, but he must slide directly into the bag. If he cannot reach second base laterally in his slide, then both runners are automatically out.

3-38. When the pitcher starts the double play, the middle infielder must round off and face the pitcher when making the pivot.

When the pitcher or catcher starts the double play and the second baseman is covering (coverage is established before the play begins), the second baseman rounds the bag and faces straight in toward the mound (fig. 3-38). He still puts his left foot on the bag, and the footwork is the same—rounding gives him a better angle to handle the throw and turn the double play.

PLAYING SHORTSTOP

Turning Double Plays

The shortstop must also cheat over to double-play depth whenever a double play is in order. There are five ways for the shortstop to start the double play:

1. When the ball is hit near the bag (within two or three steps), it should be easier for the shortstop to take it himself. He should step on the bag with his left foot, push off to the inside, and throw off his right foot.
2. When the ball is hit toward the bag but too far from it for him to touch the bag, he should make the underhand toss chest high to the second baseman.
3. When the ball is hit right at the shortstop or to the right so that he can get in front of it, he should use the sidearm throw. It is important that he stays down (fig. 3-39) while making this play; standing up will cost him valuable time.

3-39. The shortstop must stay down when starting a double play on a ball hit to his right.

3-40 and 3-41. On the ball hit far to the right that he must extend on, the shortstop should take his time, catch the ball with his left foot down, get the right foot down, and throw to second.

4. When the ball is hit to his right and he must extend for it (fig. 3-40), the double play is usually not possible. He must receive the ball, plant the right foot (fig. 3-41), and go for the force at second unless the ball is hit hard.

5. When the ball is hit slowly, he must make a judgment whether to go for the force at second or take the out at first. (A good shortstop should know the speed of the runners on the bases.) The second baseman must help him verbally on this play. The mechanics for any slow-hit ball apply here (see "Infield Drills").

If the ball is hit to the right side of the infield, the shortstop becomes the middle man in the double play. He should go hard for the base while facing in the direction of the player throwing the

3-42 and 3-43. When the second baseman or the first baseman starts the double play, the shortstop places his right foot near the bag, comes across to receive the ball while touching the bag at the same time, and throws to first.

ball and establish a position with his right foot just next to the bag (fig. 3-42). As the ball is thrown, he should move across the bag and receive it with both hands. The shortstop should take special care to close off his left shoulder in order to get something on the throw to first (fig. 3-43). When the pitcher or catcher starts the double play, the shortstop should round off and face directly toward the mound.

PLAYING FIRST BASE

First basemen have long been thought of as offensive players that are hidden at a defensive position where they won't hurt the club. A good defensive first baseman can be a big asset to his ball club. First basemen such as Will Clark and Mark Grace can help their teams win many games with their defensive skills. I often have watched these two practice their footwork during batting practice and work hard at digging balls out of the dirt and other plays that are difficult for first basemen.

Positioning

Most first basemen at all levels do not play deep enough with nobody on base. Playing deep increases range and still allows plenty of time to get to the base to cover for the throw. The infielders need a target to throw at, so the main thing is that the first baseman is set up only when they begin their throwing sequence—that is all that is necessary.

When a first baseman is holding a runner on base, his right foot should be against the bag and his left foot should be up the baseline (fig. 3-44). After the ball is delivered to the plate, he should bounce off to cover as much ground as possible—he should be two steps toward the middle of the diamond and be under control when the ball crosses the hitting area.

On bunt plays, the first baseman must cover his side of the field very aggressively. With a runner on first only, he must hold the runner on base and then charge hard toward the plate—this is the signal for the pitcher to deliver the ball. The bunter should be trying to bunt the ball to first in this sacrifice situation. The first baseman should listen for the catcher to call the play (throw

3-44. The first baseman places his right foot along the base while holding a runner on first base.

to first or second) and then react accordingly. Getting the runner at second is nice, but getting an out somewhere on a bunt play is mandatory.

If the runners are on first and second, the first baseman will be charging very early on bunt plays to cover the first-base line. With normal coverage, he is responsible for the first-base line and up the middle. The pitcher must break immediately and cover the third-base line, so the first baseman has to cover that additional area up the middle.

When the first baseman is playing behind the runner, either with a slow runner on first or runners on first and second, he should position himself just inside the left shoulder of the runner (fig. 3-45). When the bunt is in order, he should start inside the bag and charge when the pitcher delivers the ball to the plate.

3-45. When playing behind the runner, or with runners on first and second, the first baseman positions himself just off the inside shoulder of the runner.

Receiving Routine Throws

When the ball is hit to the infield, the first baseman should be set up when the infielder looks up to throw. If he is playing deep enough to have maximum range, it takes a real effort to get to the bag in time. His heels should be in the front of the bag with his body facing in the direction of the throw (fig. 3-46). It is important that he does not stretch until he sees the ball in flight and knows its direction—moving too early will limit his receiving range considerably.

High Throws, Wide Throws, and Low Throws to First

On high throws up the line, the first baseman must stay in fair territory and sweep the tag (fig. 3-47). Tagging into the runner (with a stiff arm) can result in severe injury. The rule of thumb is if you think the throw is off when it is up the line, go get the ball and tag the runner. On throws to the other side of first, he must think "stay on the bag," because if he comes off, the play is lost. On throws to the outfield side, the first baseman must remember that his first responsibility is to stop the ball. In parks with short backup fences the first baseman can stay on the bag longer if the

3-46. The first baseman should always face the direction of the throw and not stretch until he sees the ball in flight.

runner will not be able to advance on an overthrow. The game situation and the position of other runners also dictates how aggressive he can be (with a runner on second and two outs, for example, he cannot let the ball get past him).

3-47. When the throw is at the runner, the first baseman should use a sweep tag to avoid injury.

On throws in the dirt, he should get as low as possible as soon as possible (fig. 3-48). It is imperative that he center his body on the throw. As he receives the ball he should try to bring it into his belly button (fig. 3-49)—this gives him soft hands and a better chance to hang on to it. Trying to scoop the ball from the side (fig. 3-50) requires perfect timing and is simply a low-percentage play. It is much more efficient to line up dead center and at least block the ball if he is unable to catch it.

On throws coming from the area of home plate, the first baseman should offer an inside target. He should be aware that the catcher, the third baseman, and right-handed pitchers have a tendency to tail the ball toward the bag and into the runner. Remember, the runner must stay within the three-foot baseline and cannot run inside the line and interfere with the throw.

3-48 and 3-49. When the throw is in the dirt, the first baseman should center on the ball, get as low as possible as soon as possible, and bring the ball to the center of his body with both hands.

3-50. The first baseman who tries to catch the ball from the side is only lucky when he catches it cleanly.

The 3-6-3 Double Play

When a right-handed first baseman starts the double play he should let the position of the ball dictate his pivot selection. If the ball is hit right at him or to his right (fig. 3-51), he will generally turn clockwise to throw. If the ball takes him to his left (fig. 3-52), he will sometimes use a counterclockwise, or back-door, pivot. A

3-51. On the 3-6-3 double play, the ball hit to the right of the first baseman will allow him to pivot clockwise to make the throw to second.

3-52. When the ball takes him left, he should use the counterclockwise, or back-door, pivot.

left-handed first baseman will always pivot clockwise—or "follow his glove," as some coaches say.

The first throw in every double play is the most important one. The first baseman usually has more time than he thinks, so he should take his time and make a chest-high accurate throw. It is very important that he doesn't throw the ball directly in the baseline and into the runner. He should either charge the ball aggressively or take a step forward after receiving the ball to avoid throwing in the baseline and possibly hitting the runner. On many balls hit to his right, the first baseman will not be able to get back to the bag, so the pitcher must be there to take the return throw from the shortstop.

The Pitcher Covering First

The first baseman who plays deep must rely on the pitcher to cover on a good many grounders to the right side. On balls fielded near the bag, he should make the tag himself, making sure to wave off the pitcher in time for him to stay out of the play. But on grounders fielded too far from the bag to make the unassisted play, he should give the pitcher a firm, letter-high, underhand leading toss. Ground balls hit toward the second-base hole often require an overhand throw to the pitcher covering, but it still should be a leading, chest-high toss—throws below the waist to a pitcher trying to step on the bag are very difficult to handle.

On push bunts and short ground balls, the first baseman should always charge the ball. The pitcher is trained to stay on his route and continue to the bag to receive the throw if he can't field the ball himself.

Pop-Up Responsibilities

The first baseman has a lot of ground to cover on pop-ups. Coming in, he needs to be very aggressive in both fair and foul territory. Going back, in foul territory he should be aggressive, but in fair territory the second baseman should provide considerable help. The first baseman should always be aware of the positioning of the second baseman in order to better anticipate his own coverage—the second baseman has a much better angle on the ball. (See Chapter 8 for complete coverage responsibilities.)

PLAYING THIRD BASE

The mechanics of playing third base are the same as those for the other infield positions, but it takes a special ballplayer to play third well. Many times, the third baseman will need to block hard-hit balls to keep them in front of him (fig. 3-53). A good third baseman can also save his team many runs by becoming skilled at fielding balls hit down the line (fig. 3-54). This backhand play is one of the most difficult that a third baseman can make.

3-53. A good third baseman can block hard-hit balls in the dirt and will sacrifice his body for the team.

3-54. Fielding balls down the line and making the long throw to first is a very difficult play for even the best major league third basemen.

The third baseman is responsible for the greatest variance in positioning of any infielder. He must read the game situation constantly and adjust his position accordingly. With a player at the plate who can run, he must protect against the bunt but not give up too much range by assuming that a bunt for a base hit is coming. With two strikes on the hitter, the third baseman can assume that the bunt will not be attempted and move back to regular depth. (If the hitter tries to bunt for a base hit with two strikes, let him try it.)

The third baseman will get the strangest topped balls from right-handed hitters and balls that spin funny from left-handed hitters. He will get short-hop rockets hit at his feet and will have to make very long throws at times. It takes a smart, tough, and agile player with a strong arm to play third base.

COACHES' CORNER: INFIELD DRILLS

Drill 1—Slow-Hit Balls

A coach has very little chance to work on slow-hit balls with his infielders during practices. But sooner or later it will happen: with the game on the line the pitcher will make a good pitch and jam a hitter and he will dribble the ball—and nobody can make the play. Why? Because you haven't worked on it for several weeks. A smart coach doesn't leave it up to the players to work on all the plays.

Set up your infield at the beginning or end of practice. Have the first baseman just cover the bag, as he will only receive throws during this drill (he will get some throws that are not pretty, so he can work on the tough throws in the dirt and up the line both ways). Hit slow-hit balls at each infielder. Make the plays easy at first and then progressively more difficult as the drill continues. You may use two first basemen or even two sets of infielders and rotate them in and out. You can get in 10 rounds within 6 or 7 minutes, stop and discuss it, then get in 10 more rounds, all within 15 minutes. You will need a bucket of balls next to you and an empty bucket by the first baseman—he simply places the balls in the bucket when he catches them. The catchers can shag the balls for you. This drill done twice a week will really help develop these skills. Note: Before you do this or any other drill, make sure you have taught the infielders the mechanics of the play and that they have had some success doing it one-on-one with you at a slower rate. You don't want players practicing any skill in an incorrect manner. This drill can be lots of fun for you and the players.

Drill 2—Double Plays

Nothing will bail a team out of a jam better than a good old double play. Winning teams are generally above average in turning double plays. Infielders can work on their double plays during batting practice, but I've found that doing it once a week or so at the beginning or at the end of practice in a different setting has added value. It provides me with an opportunity to watch them more closely (there are lots of things going on during batting practice), and I can also compare my players and evaluate them better.

Without using baserunners, set up an infield and tell them that every ball you hit is a double-play ball. Using the same setup as Drill 1 (a bucket of balls at home and an empty bucket at first), hit one ball after another to each infielder in turn and have them turn double plays. The first baseman should alternate between holding an imaginary runner on first and playing behind him. You have the option of putting a pitcher on the mound to work on not only comebackers and the 1-6-3 double play but the 3-6-1 double play as well. I always have fun with this one; my challenge is always "Turn ten in a row perfect, and we are done." You may also have someone keep time and make them turn every double play in 4.4 seconds or less (the average time in the majors for a runner to reach first). This drill should take less than 15 minutes (50 double plays). Again, make sure beforehand that the players understand the mechanics of the play.

Drill 3—Fielding Practice for Pitchers

Place your pitching staff on the mound and the first baseman at first. You will need at least three players to play first base, so use outfielders or third basemen. The shortstop and second baseman should also be in position.

Begin with balls hit at the first baseman that he tosses to the pitcher covering. Mix in some in-between plays where the first baseman and the pitcher must decide who takes the ball and who goes to the bag. Include some balls hit back to the pitcher (remember—they must know who is covering second before the play starts) and some 3-6-1 double plays. You can work some bunt plays into this drill, or you may want to work on them separately, as in Drill 4.

Within a 15-minute period, you can touch on all the plays necessary, but in order to do this drill properly you will need 20–30 minutes of practice time.

Drill 4—Team Bunt Defense

On this drill you can use the outfielders and extra pitchers as baserunners. (They should wear helmets.) Place half of them at third and half at first. Put your entire infield in place and one pitcher at a time on the mound.

Counting the squeeze, there are three basic bunts to defense: the sacrifice bunt with a runner on first and less than two outs, the bunt with runners on first and second with no outs, and the squeeze bunt with a runner on third and one out. Remember that you must explain the responsibilities of each player in detail before you can expect the players to react to the game situations.

With the defense in place and runners ready at the appropriate bases, call out the game situation and roll or hit the bunt. After the play, evaluate their performance: Did they throw the ball to the proper base? Did they communicate well? Did they cover their areas of responsibility in the proper manner? If not, correct them, put a different pitcher on the mound, and go again. Pay special attention to positioning and communication. (A suggestion: don't yell out where to throw the ball—make them do it.)

In a period of 15 minutes or so you can cover all the plays, and the players will have fun and learn to react to the ball and the game situations that you describe to them.

Drill 5—Defending the Double Steal

Put your entire infield in place and position baserunners to attempt the double steal. The more realistic you can make this drill the more valuable it will be. Make sure the runners run at nearly full speed and that players throw as they would in game situations. Timing is so important on this play—if everyone goes at half-speed, it is a waste of time.

Begin the drill with the pitcher throwing the ball to the catcher and the catcher (depending on the play that has been called) throwing the ball to the appropriate base.

Arrange ahead of time the offensive play that you want the runners to execute. I suggest that you coach third and put the plays on from there. If you have a bright catcher (for your sake, I hope you do), let him mix up the plays and try them all. Have the runner on third break early, late, and any other time to try to disrupt the defense. Also, make the pitcher get the pitching signs from the catcher—the runner on third may get him to balk by breaking early (better now than in a game).

The drill should last about 20 minutes. If you have only one catcher throwing, you should shut it down after 20 throws or so. Make sure to have some of the runners from first stop and get into rundowns.

Drill 6—Defensing the Rundown

This drill can be a lot of fun for the team. Place your entire infield on the field and use the outfielders and extra pitchers as base-runners.

Start the drill by having the pitcher pick a runner off first base. Then follow with pickoffs at every base. You can cover all of the rundown situations in 10 minutes or so. This drill can also be done as part of or following the bunt drill. The team must thoroughly understand rundown execution; these skills must be taught in small groups or individually. (See Chapter 8 for defensive assignments on rundowns.)

Drill 7—Team Pop-Up Coverage

Refer to Chapter 8 for the pop-up responsibilities for each player. A chalk talk is a necessity before any drill of this kind. The mechanics of the play should be discussed in detail. Communication is essential—a lack of it can not only lose games but cause serious injuries. With my players I always start off by throwing the ball from the mound and working with them two at a time—one infielder and one outfielder (yes, even pro players).

Next, set up your entire defense—infield and outfield—and hit the pop-up between the infielders at random using a machine. Most coaches can't hit pop-ups very well. Even the best can't drop the ball in between the infield and the outfield consistently enough to make the drill move quickly. Nothing is worse than having 20 players stand around watching a coach trying to find his pop-up stroke. Don't be stubborn—use a pitching machine and the drill will move quickly, the pop-ups will be perfect, and the club will have fun doing it. This drill should take no more than 15 minutes.

4
THE CATCHER: TEAM LEADER

If someone were starting a team tomorrow, the first thing they should do is acquire a good catcher. Over the years, very few teams have won championships without a fine catcher. The catcher must be a team leader, direct the efforts of the pitchers, and in many ways become an extension of the coach. He must be enthusiastic, durable, dependable, and must display a positive attitude at all times.

A good catcher should work with his pitchers and develop a personal relationship with each one of them. He must quickly learn which ones to chew out and which ones to stroke in order to get the most out of each pitcher. The catcher must find out which ones are weak emotionally and which ones are strong—the weak will need constant attention, while the strong usually can be left alone. The catcher must learn the delivery of each pitcher and be able to tell when something is wrong. Every pitching coach should use his catchers to help the pitchers understand game situations, pitch sequences, and basic mechanics.

Qualities of a good catcher:

- Is a team leader
- Has a positive attitude

- Is an enthusiastic player every day of the season
- Is tough, durable, and dependable
- Works well with his pitchers
- Has a great relationship with his coach
- Gets along well with umpires
- Has a professional approach to the game at all times

There are never enough good defensive catchers. The position requires exceptional athletic skills and a special attitude and love of the game. Most players simply aren't willing to pay the price.

A catcher should use a lightweight, flexible glove—he can't "grow into" a glove. He must be able to receive the ball and get it out his glove quickly and easily. The chest protector, shin guards, and mask should be of good quality and fit well. A protective cup and a catcher's helmet are musts, and a throat guard is a very good idea.

RECEIVING THE BALL

When the catcher is giving signs to the pitcher, he should hold his glove hand in a position that will prevent the third-base coach from seeing the signs (fig. 4-1) and his right knee in a position that will prevent the first-base coach from seeing them (fig. 4-2). All the pitchers on each pitching staff should use the same signs. The infielders will need to know what pitch is coming, so continuity is important. When there is a man on second, a series of signs is necessary; major leaguers usually give three signs and use the middle or last sign in the sequence. The catcher should try to keep the signs simple—cross-ups can be very costly.

After he gives the signs, the catcher shifts to the ready, or receiving, position (fig. 4-3). He can walk into this position by moving his left foot and then the right, or he may hop into this position with a small jump to get the feet set. The right foot should be three or four inches behind the left (fig. 4-4) to allow for freedom of movement and quickness. The thighs should be parallel to the ground and the back straight but not stiff. The glove hand should be extended out in front of the knees (fig. 4-5) and not trapped between them (fig. 4-6). The bare hand should be behind the catcher, protected from foul tips (fig. 4-7), when there are no baserunners; with runners on base, the hand should be next to the

4-1. When the catcher is giving the signs, the glove blocks the view of the third-base coach.

4-2. Closing up the right knee will stop the first-base coach from seeing the signs.

4-3. After giving the signs, the catcher shifts to the ready, or receiving, position.

4-4. Note that the toe of the right foot lines up with the instep of the left foot.

4-5. The catcher must extend his glove hand out and away from the body for freedom of movement.

4-6. Catchers who lock their elbows cannot receive pitches smoothly, especially pitches out of the strike zone.

4-7. With nobody on base, the catcher should place his bare hand behind his back in order to protect it from foul tips.

glove with the fingers relaxed and curled (see fig. 4-3). The catcher's weight should be slightly forward and on the balls of the feet. This position might seem awkward at first but will become comfortable with time. A catcher must be able to move in either direction quickly, and this position enables him to do this easily.

The catcher must give the pitcher a good target at all times. Young catchers should set up down the middle early in the count and not ask an inexperienced pitcher to do something he can't do by setting up on corners until they are ahead in the count.

THROWING THE BALL

A catcher's defensive value and ability is based for the most part on how he throws to the bases. The other parts of the catcher's game are important, but throwing is the measuring stick by which his peers and opponents will judge his defense.

Throwing accurately depends on a combination of preparation and mechanics. The first step in preparation is to be comfortable in the receiving stance. Also, the catcher should be alert with runners on base in order to react properly when a throwing situation develops. A catcher should never watch the flight of the ball when he throws; instead, he should watch the target all the way. Many players watch the ball in flight (catchers and infielders) and this hurts their overall accuracy.

Pickoff Plays to First Base

Pickoff plays to first base can be initiated by the catcher, the first baseman, or the manager. A pick and rub is the usual method of signaling a pickoff move, although a spontaneous play with the first baseman breaking is also possible.

If the catcher desires, he can pitch out and run the pickoff to first or other bases. Sometimes the count on the hitter won't allow a pitchout, so a pitch on the outside part of the plate is the next best thing. If the pitch is not a good pitch to throw on, the catcher should abort the pickoff attempt.

The catcher must stay low and move his right foot even before receiving the ball (fig. 4-8). He should close off his upper body by moving both hands up to the top of the letters (fig. 4-9) and then step in the direction of first base and make the throw (fig. 4-10). It is important that he doesn't come out too soon or pop up and block the umpire's view of the pitch.

Pitchouts

On pitchouts the catcher should step into the opposite batter's box after the pitcher starts to the plate (fig. 4-11). If the catcher jumps out early, it is a balk. The ball should be thrown letter high, but the catcher must be prepared for poor pitchouts. A catcher must be careful not to overthrow on pitchouts.

Throwing to Second Base

When a runner tries to steal second, the first baseman must help out the catcher by letting him know the runner is going. The catcher will see the runner break with a right-handed hitter at the plate. With a left-handed hitter he will often not see the break, but

4-8, 4-9, and 4-10. On throws to first, the catcher should move his right foot, close off his upper body by raising his hands to his chest, and make the throw while stepping toward first base.

4-11. On pitchouts, the catcher should get into the opposite batter's box and provide a good target.

he still should anticipate the situation and be prepared to throw.

When the pitch is down the middle or to the outside, the catcher should take a small step forward at approximately a 45-degree angle (fig. 4-12). After he receives the ball, he then should bring the ball (with both hands) up to the letters to close off the upper body (fig. 4-13) and throw with a controlled step toward second and the target (fig. 4-14). The catcher should remain as low as possible during these movements and be careful not to block out the umpire and cost his pitcher a strike.

If the pitch is inside to a right-handed hitter, the catcher must take a small step with his left foot to center the ball (fig. 4-15), transfer his weight quickly to his right foot as he closes off the upper body (fig. 4-16), and take a controlled step toward the target. This left-right-left movement is called the "shift" method.

4-12, 4-13, and 4-14. When the pitch is down the middle or to the outside, the catcher should center the ball, close off his front side by raising his hands to his chest, and step toward second base and throw.

4-15 and 4-16. On balls in on a right-handed hitter, the catcher should take a small step with his left foot to center the ball, close off, and throw to second (the hitter must get out of the catcher's way or be called for interference).

Taking a controlled step toward the target is important—if the catcher jumps or steps too far, his back leg will break down and he will feel as if he is throwing uphill. High throws into center field will usually be the result. Keeping his head on a straight line toward the target will help his overall accuracy.

Throwing to Third Base

When a runner steals third, it is almost always the pitcher who is at fault. Stealing third can be easier than stealing second for an accomplished baserunner who is allowed to take a big lead. If the pitcher sees that the runner has moved too far off base or has taken a walking lead, he must step off the rubber and not deliver the ball to the plate.

With a left-handed hitter at the plate, some catchers throwing to third like to take a small step with their right foot to gain

4-17 and 4-18. When throwing to third on pitches away, the catcher should throw in front of the hitter.

momentum and step directly at the ball (fig. 4-17). More and more catchers are simply receiving the ball while shifting their weight to the right foot and throwing without moving their right foot.

With a right-handed hitter at the plate, the catcher must decide whether to throw in front of or behind the hitter. The direction of the pitch will dictate which way to go. Some major league catchers set up in their receiving stance a little deeper in the catcher's box to get a better view of third base.

When the pitch is outside, the catcher should throw in front of the hitter by taking a step forward with his right foot, then stepping toward third with the left foot (fig. 4-18). If the pitch is on the inside, the catcher should throw behind the hitter. Remember that the hitter moves forward toward the pitcher when he strides—this makes the throw for the catcher easier than it appears. The first move is to the side with the left foot (fig. 4-19), followed by a shifting of the weight to the right foot (fig. 4-20), and then stepping to third with the left foot (fig. 4-21).

4-19, 4-20, and 4-21. When the pitch is inside, the catcher should take a small step with the left foot to center, bring the right foot back, and throw behind the hitter (the hitter has taken a stride and moved forward).

The First-and-Third Double Steal

When a team attempts to steal second with men on first and third, the catcher must assume that a double steal is a possibility. He should first check the runner on third as he closes off his front shoulder (fig. 4-22) before stepping toward second to throw. If the runner on third has broken for the plate, then the catcher will throw to third or start a rundown to get the lead runner. If the runner on third breaks as the ball is on its way to second, the shortstop or second baseman should come forward to catch the ball and throw it back to home for the tag.

Throwing—Points to Remember

- Don't rush—it will likely result in a mishandled ball or inaccurate throw.
- Practice footwork slowly at first to gain consistency.

4-22. When the offense attempts a double steal (with runners on first and third), the catcher should check the runner at third and then throw through to second.

- Stay as low as possible while making throws to the bases.
- Close off your front side or your shoulder will open too soon.
- Watch the target and not the ball in flight.
- Trying to throw too hard will cause a major breakdown in mechanics and accuracy.
- The stride is a small, controlled step—don't jump.

4-23. The catcher should position his anchor foot so that he gives the runner a place to slide.

THE TAG AT HOME PLATE

Even though the catcher wears protective equipment, he still risks serious injury if he applies the tag improperly. The runner will be charging in at full speed, and in any collision both the runner and the catcher can be hurt. Most catchers take their masks off to make the tag, but it is perfectly acceptable to leave it on.

The catcher must learn to block the plate in order to make an effective tag. He must give the runner some of the plate to slide toward; otherwise, the runner's only choice will be to run over the catcher. He should plant his left foot, the anchor foot, approximately 18 inches in front of the plate with the toes pointing toward third base (fig. 4-23). *It is extremely important that this anchor foot is pointed directly at the runner as he makes contact with the catcher. If the catcher's leg is at an angle (fig. 4-24), the impact could tear the interior or exterior ligaments of the catcher's knee.*

4-24. If the catcher's foot is at an angle, the runner can do serious damage to the catcher's left knee.

4-25. As he receives the ball (or just before he receives it), the catcher should assume the blocking position by moving the left foot to take away the plate from the runner. Notice that the left toe is pointing up the line toward the runner. The ball should be gripped in the bare hand when the tag is applied.

As the catcher receives the ball (the runner has committed to the slide at this point) he should move his left foot to block the plate entirely (fig. 4-25). As he applies the tag, he should grip the ball in his bare hand and always turn the back of his glove toward the runner to avoid injury to the inside of his wrist. The runner

4-26. The catcher then drives the shin guard down on the runner, preventing him from reaching the plate.

will slide into the catcher's shin guard before reaching the plate (fig. 4-26). After making the tag, the catcher should alertly look around for another play.

If the throw is slightly off line, the catcher can move the right foot, or pivot foot, to the ball without leaving the solid tagging position. Of course, if the throw is too far off line, the catcher must leave the tagging position and get the ball.

If the runner comes in standing up, the catcher should make the tag but try to avoid a head-on collision by rolling away from the runner. As always, he should apply the tag with the back of his glove facing the runner. When the throw arrives, the ball should be placed in the bare hand and the runner should be tagged with the back of the glove.

Making the tag at the plate

- Your initial position should show the runner some of the plate.
- Hold the ball in your bare hand when applying the tag.
- As you catch the ball, move your anchor foot so that it blocks the plate entirely.
- Your left foot must point directly at the runner to avoid injury.
- Avoid head-on collisions—runner and catcher both lose.
- After the tag, be alert for another play.

4-27. When blocking the ball straight ahead, the catcher drops to both knees, protects his bare hand, and tucks his chin on his chest to protect his throat.

4-28. He must overcome the natural tendency to try to catch the ball.

BLOCKING PITCHES IN THE DIRT

Every pitcher will throw pitches in the dirt during the course of the game, and few catchers can block them all. One of the keys is anticipation: when the pitcher throws a curveball, for example, the catcher should look for the ball to be down.

The ball in the middle is the easiest to block: simply drop to both knees facing the ball (fig. 4-27). The chin must be tucked, and the catcher must avoid the natural tendency to try to catch the ball with the glove (fig. 4-28)—the glove should protect the groin area while stopping the ball from escaping through the legs. He should lean forward so that his upper body hovers over the ball—this movement will prevent it from rolling too far away after it is blocked. The chances are that if the ball is blocked and rolls only a short distance in front of the plate, the runners will not advance.

When blocking pitches to either side, the catcher should use basically the same blocking positions; the difference is in the initial movements. To go to the left to block, he should push off his right leg (fig. 4-29) and drop to both knees (fig. 4-30). To block a ball to the right, he should drive off his left leg (fig. 4-31) and get in position (fig. 4-32). Note that the angle of the body blocks the ball back to the center of the diamond. Curveballs will bounce laterally and sometimes bounce up on the catcher—he must do an extra-special job of hovering on this pitch.

4-29 and 4-30. On balls to his left, the catcher drives off his right leg and blocks the ball back toward the middle of the field (note the angle of the shoulders).

4-31 and 4-32. When the ball is hit to the right, he drives off his left leg and blocks the ball back toward the plate.

After he blocks the ball, the catcher should get to his feet, get rid of his mask, and prepare to throw if a runner is attempting to advance. A failure to block a ball at a critical time can put a runner in scoring position, allow him to go to third, or score a run. (Remember—the catcher must be prepared to block a ball with two strikes on a hitter and nobody on base.) Even letting a runner advance to second in the first inning can cost the ball club the game. The skill of blocking can't be developed without long hours of practice. A catcher should start with blocking tennis balls until the movements have been developed. The pain comes with the job—there are no shortcuts.

There is no greater feeling for a catcher than to block a tough curveball in the dirt with a runner on third in the last inning of a tight game. Catching is by far the most difficult position, and blocking balls is the single toughest skill to master.

Blocking balls in the dirt

- Start with a balanced position.
- Anticipate the ball in the dirt.
- Drop to both knees and assume the proper angle.
- Center on the ball with the chest protector.
- Tuck the chin for throat protection.
- Lean over the ball with the upper body.
- When blocking to the side, drive off the opposite leg.
- Resist the tendency to try to catch the ball and keep the glove on the ground.

POP-UPS, BUNTS, AND CUTOFFS

Every catcher needs an effective method for catching pop-ups. The ball will come off the bat spinning violently and will curve back toward the field. When the ball goes up, the catcher should turn his back to the field and face the backstop (fig. 4-33). As the ball rises, he should give chase with his mask in his hand. When the ball reaches its highest point and he recognizes exactly where it will come down, he may toss his mask away. He should catch the ball over his head with two hands (fig. 4-34). (Refer to Chapter 8 for pop-up coverage responsibilities.)

When the ball is bunted in front of the plate, the catcher is in the best position to field it and make an accurate throw. When the ball is anywhere in the catcher's area of responsibility, he should call for the ball loudly, stay low, and scoop it up with both hands (fig. 4-35). If the ball is out of his area, he should help direct traffic, call the player who is to field the bunt, and tell him where to throw it.

The catcher is the captain of the defense and must know the

4-33 and 4-34. On pop-ups, the catcher should turn his back to the field, find the ball, get rid of his mask, and catch the ball with both hands above his head.

4-35. On bunt plays, the catcher should round the ball and scoop it into the glove with both hands.

game situation at all times in order to direct the efforts of the infielders on cutoffs and relays. Most teams use a simple system of voice communication ("Cut!" and "Relay!"). It is very important that the catcher not let unnecessary throws come through to the plate, particularly if such throws allow baserunners to advance.

HELPING THE PITCHER GET HITTERS OUT

Most pitchers don't think well on the mound and need help in tough situations. They get flustered when things don't go well for them; they battle the umpire and lose mechanics as they overthrow their pitches. The catcher must be able to settle down a pitcher when he is losing emotional control.

Catchers must be able to spot differences in individual hitters, pick out their weaknesses, and work to get them out. All hitters hit for a higher average when they are ahead in the count, so the first pitch or two to a hitter are very important. The catcher should set up in the middle of the plate early in the count to get more strikes. The pitcher and catcher must work together, but the ultimate decision for pitch selection rests with the pitcher.

Catchers should study Chapter 2, especially the section called "Calling Your Own Game: When and How to Use Your Pitches."

COACHES' CORNER: CATCHING DRILLS

Drill 1—Footwork Drill

Catchers need to develop quick feet. Jumping rope is great for conditioning and quickness. An ongoing flexibility program is also important for catchers who look forward to long and competitive careers.

To improve footwork, catchers can do the following drill for 5 or 10 minutes at the end of nearly every practice without any danger to their throwing arms.

Two catchers should position themselves 50 feet apart facing each other with full equipment (including mask) in place. The object is to throw the ball back and forth for 20 consecutive throws without dropping the ball, moving the ball to alternating sides as they throw to each another. In other words, catcher one throws just off catcher two's left shoulder; catcher two must move his feet to center the ball. He returns the ball to catcher one's left shoulder; he also must adjust his feet and get in front of (center) the throw. Catcher one throws the next time to catcher two's right shoulder, and so on. If the ball is dropped, or if a catcher fails to center a throw, the drill is stopped and the count to 20 begins again.

In addition to quickening the feet, helping throwing accuracy, and making the hands more sure, this drill is a great conditioner for the catchers. Twenty throws doesn't sound like much, but remember that the catchers are working at full speed with full gear. Check to make sure that they close off their upper bodies as they throw.

Drill 2—Throwing to the Bases

Pitch from just in front of the mound and have each catcher make five or six throws to each base. When they throw to first, place a hitter in the left-handed batter's box; when they throw to third, place him in the right-handed batter's box; and when they throw to second, alternate the hitter's positioning.

Pay special attention to mechanics as the catchers are throwing to the bases. If necessary, stand next to the catcher and have someone else pitch. Make sure to mix up the pitches—some up in the zone, some down, some in, and some out. It also is a good idea to mix speeds and throw some breaking stuff for each catcher to handle. This entire drill should last no more than 10 minutes.

Drill 3—Blocking Pitches in the Dirt

I recommend using tennis balls or a soft version of a baseball when doing this drill—catchers don't need to get beaten up any more than necessary. But at the end of each session it's okay to use a real baseball for a few throws. Young catchers learning to block must spend several minutes of every practice working on technique. This is one skill in which fundamentals are everything.

Throw to the catcher from a distance of about 50 feet. This is far enough from the catcher for him to react to the ball and to make the drill seem realistic. Throw three or four straight at him at first; then tell him which side you are going to throw to. Finally, don't tell him which way you are going to throw the ball and check his reactions. Throw an occasional strike to see if he is leaning too soon.

A coach can make this drill fun by challenging the catchers to keep the ball inside the circle of the dirt around home plate. Don't let the drill go on so long that it becomes a negative experience. A special relationship with your catchers is very important—use the time with them in a productive manner.

5
PLAYING THE OUTFIELD

In Little Leagues all over the country the worst players get stuck in the outfield. They usually are just not good enough to pitch or play in the infield, and at the lower levels of baseball the coaches hide them on defense. But the higher you go up the baseball ladder, the more important outfielders become. In the major leagues the best team in the division almost always has one of the best all-around outfields.

Many outfielders in the major leagues don't have strong throwing arms but develop the ability to charge the ball and make quick, accurate throws. Outfielders with less than average speed who are aggressive and take the proper angle will cut off hits in the gap and save their teams many runs over the course of the season. Outfielders with just average speed who position themselves well will make plays that others with great speed who play out of position won't. At the higher levels of baseball, the outfielders have a terrific defensive impact on whether a team wins or loses.

OUTFIELD POSITIONING

Good outfielders position themselves according to the game situation. Below the Double-A level of professional baseball, pitchers have trouble "pitching" to hitters or hitting the spots. Most out-fielders at these levels are better off just playing straight away on nearly all hitters: the leftfielder lined up with first base and second base, the rightfielder lined up with second base and third base, and the centerfielder two or three steps to either side of the pitcher (he can't see the hitter from directly behind the pitcher).

When the tying run is on second late in the game, the out-fielders must play shallow enough to throw the runner out at the plate on a routine single. If the tying run is on first late in the game, the outfielders should play deep enough that a fly ball cannot get over their heads. Some coaches call this position "no doubles."

A good outfielder also plays the count. If a hitter is in the hole—no balls and two strikes—the outfielders should move in a couple of steps and maybe even a couple steps to the opposite field. When a hitter is behind in the count like this, he is more apt to protect the plate and less likely to drive the ball. Conversely, with counts like 2-0 and 3-1, the outfielders should move back a step or two, for the hitter is very aggressive on these counts and is more likely to hit the ball with authority.

With pull hitters, the centerfielder should play 4–6 steps toward the gap; the other outfielders should make a similar adjust-ment. With opposite-field hitters, the outfielders should adjust their positions toward the opposite field.

BACKING UP PLAYS

As the old saying goes, "The outfielders ought to be the most tired players on the field when the game is over." There are very few defensive plays that don't require some kind of backup from the outfielders. They need to back up each other, back up the in-fielders, and back up the bases. When an outfielder is late backing up, it usually goes unnoticed by most, but this laziness will cost a team many games over the course of the season. A pet peeve of most coaches is when the overthrow to second by the catcher goes into center field and the runner advances to third. If the center-fielder breaks forward as soon as the ball passes the hitter, the basestealer should never get to third on this play unless the ball is deflected by the middle infielder or slowed by long grass in the outfield.

5-1. When no throw is in order, the outfielder should center on the ball.

THROWING FROM THE OUTFIELD

Fielding Ground Balls

On ground balls with the bases empty, the outfielder should center the ball (fig. 5-1). He must always know the baserunner's speed—the game situation will dictate how aggressive the runner will be.

When an outfielder has to make a throw, he must charge the ball aggressively. As he approaches the ball, he should take short, choppy steps and "break down" to gain body control and balance. He should field the ball on his glove side with the glove foot (left foot for a right-handed player) down (fig. 5-2), "crow hop" while closing off his upper body (fig. 5-3), stride with his left foot, and throw (fig. 5-4). All outfielders should try to throw with the cross-seam grip (fig. 5-5). This grip provides for a true flight and better distance on the throw.

Before the play begins, *all* defensive players must anticipate that the ball will be hit to them. They should also think about where they will throw the ball if it is. One of the key goals of team defense is to keep opposing runners out of scoring position. A good, low-trajectory throw from the outfielder to the cutoff man will usually force the runner to stop at first base.

5-2, 5-3, and 5-4. When a throw is in order, a right-handed outfielder should field the ball with his left foot down, crow hop to close off the upper body, and throw the ball over the top with a good follow-through.

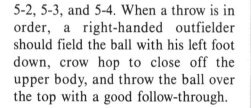

5-5. All outfielders should throw with a cross-seam, or four-seam, grip.

Catching Fly Balls

One of the most important things about catching fly balls is setting up to throw as quickly as possible. The outfielder must maintain a position behind the ball at all times in order to have some forward momentum as he catches the ball. Catch the ball with both hands over the throwing shoulder (fig. 5-6) with the

5-6 and 5-7. Outfielders should try to catch every ball over the throwing shoulder and take a crow hop to close off the front side.

right foot forward (for right-handers), "crow hop" while closing the shoulders and hips (fig. 5-7), and follow with an aggressive move through the ball to throw. Keep your head moving and extend directly toward your target.

Outfielders must not interrupt their momentum during this sequence of movements. These skills can only be developed with practice at a slower speed to emphasize the high level of balance and body control that they require.

A Great Drill for Fly Balls and Throwing Accuracy

Begin by tossing balls in the air a very short distance (fig. 5-8) and have the outfielder throw 50 or 60 feet. When he becomes very comfortable with the mechanics, gradually increase the distance and height of your tosses and the distance that the outfielder must throw the ball. You also can move the player from side to side, in and back. Remind him to throw with the cross-seam grip. Depending on the age and experience of the player, several sessions of 15–20 minutes each will be required to develop balance, body control, and arm accuracy.

5-8. A coach can begin to train outfielders to catch the ball properly by tossing balls up in the air a short distance and moving back as they become skilled in the proper mechanics.

Drifting to the Ball

Most outfielders try to drift to the ball or "time" the catch. When this happens, they are rarely in position to make a throw. When the ball is hit, the player should hustle over, staying behind the ball at all times and therefore keeping the ball in front of him. It is a very good idea for an outfielder to try to catch every ball as if a throw is in order. This will not only build good habits but may save him if the ball gets caught in the wind or if he misjudges the ball. The player who hustles to the ball and sets up properly will be able to make these last-second adjustments.

BALLS HIT IN THE GAPS

The one thing that must happen on plays in the gap is that one outfielder must take the short angle and go for the ball (try to cut it off) and the other must take the deep angle to back him up. When both outfielders go for the ball and no one backs up the play, the ball often ends up going all the way to the wall; even worse, a collision is a distinct possibility. When both outfielders take the deep angle, there is no one to cut the ball off.

Teams must adopt a system of vocal and hand signals that every player understands and uses. The centerfielder should take the leadership role in communicating with his fellow outfielders. He must be very aggressive and vocal on every ball hit in either gap. If the ball is an equal distance from two outfielders, the centerfielder will usually go for the ball and the leftfielder or rightfielder will back him up.

COMING IN ON BALLS

Diving for the ball on plays in the gap is a relatively low-risk move. When a player extends to either side (see the section called "Diving for Balls" in Chapter 3), he rarely gets hurt unless he runs into another player. However, when a player dives straight ahead he can easily dislocate his shoulder or suffer other injuries. But even worse when an infielder going back collides with an outfielder diving straight ahead: in the 1970s a leftfielder in the Carolina League died as a result of diving straight ahead for a ball and colliding headfirst with the knee of the shortstop going back on the ball.

It is much safer for an outfielder to slide for a ball exactly like he is sliding into a base. He will keep the ball in front of him more often, and the chances of injuries are greatly diminished.

GOING BACK ON BALLS

By far the most difficult skill an outfielder must develop is going back on balls over his head. At least a third of all major league outfielders have not fully developed this skill and at times make poor plays going back. For whatever reason—overemphasis on offense, lack of instruction in the early years—outfielders at all levels are just not as good as they should be at going back.

When a player goes back on the ball he should use a drop step—to the right when the ball is hit over his right shoulder (fig. 5-9) and to the left when it is hit over his left shoulder (fig. 5-10). After the drop step, the outfielder should cross over (fig. 5-11) and stay sideways on the ball while going back. If he turns and faces the ball while still moving backward, he will get into the back-pedal position (fig. 5-12). From this position he will have no speed,

5-9. When the ball is hit over the right shoulder, the outfielder uses a drop-step right.

5-10. If the ball is hit over the left shoulder, he uses a drop-step left.

5-11. After the drop step, the outfielder should use a crossover step.

5-12. Outfielders should avoid the backpedal position at all times. A player has no balance, speed, or leaping ability from this position.

no balance, and, since he is back on his heels, will not see the ball clearly or be able to jump. If the outfielder approaches the wall and is still going back, he must count on the outfielder next to him to help him out.

The bottom line is that all defensive players must help each other out. Nothing is more important than communication for the team defense concept to work.

PLAYING THE SUN

All defensive players must learn to deal with the sun. At the professional level, some players count on sunglasses alone to do the job. Unless a defensive player learns to use his glove and other techniques, he will never be able to handle the most difficult plays in the sun.

Some fly balls and pop-ups will pass through the sun twice— once on the way up and again on the way down. As a player waits between pitches, he must determine where to raise his glove so that it will block out the sunlight. A common mistake players make is looking up immediately when the ball is hit and finding themselves staring directly into the sun (fig. 5-13). If the glove

5-13. A player who doesn't know exactly where to put his glove will get an eyeful of sun when he looks up for the ball.

5-14. If the player has checked the sun regularly during the game, he will successfully block the sun from his eyes and catch the ball.

5-15. Getting a side angle on the ball can help a player see the ball better.

comes up first, this may not happen to the player who knows exactly where to hold the glove (fig. 5-14).

Another possibility is to stand to the side (fig. 5-15) and get a different angle on the ball. Often a player who comes in from a different angle will have no trouble with the sun at all. If the player trying to catch the ball is having lots of trouble, he should let everyone know immediately so that someone else can call him off the ball. Catching balls in the sun is very difficult and requires lots of practice (please refer to Drill 2 in the "Coaches' Corner" section).

COACHES' CORNER: OUTFIELD DRILLS

Drill 1—Fly Balls over the Head

This drill should be done regularly with all of your players with the exception of the catchers and pitchers. Without a doubt this is the skill that baseball players at all levels are the worst at. After explaining the mechanics of the play, line up a group of no more than six or seven players in the middle of the field. Begin by telling them drop step right and then throwing the ball over the right shoulders. After a couple of rounds, switch to the left. After a few successful turns by each player (staying sideways on the ball and not backpedaling), stop telling them which way that you intend to throw the ball and make them simply react. Players must learn the proper mechanics of this play if they are ever going to be efficient at going back on balls.

The next step is to toss the ball high and straight over their heads and make them decide which drop step to use. They must learn to turn away from the ball to right themselves if they turn the wrong way. In other words, if the outfielder turns to the left and uses a drop step left and then discovers that the ball is in fact over his right shoulder, he must turn counterclockwise to right himself. If he turns clockwise he will end up backpedaling for several steps and lose all speed and balance. Sure, it means taking your eye off the ball for an instant—but if you don't react this way you will never get to the tough-to-get balls.

Drill 2—Fly Balls into the Sun

If a player has developed a procedure for blocking with his glove, he can be successful catching 90 percent of balls in the sun. But most players don't know how to approach these balls.

I always start with a soft version of the baseball (even for professional players) because nobody has much confidence without a system for making these tough plays. Players will tell you "I know—you block the sun with your glove"; but they soon find out that it is not as easy as it sounds.

Begin the drill by tossing the ball just 30 or 40 feet in the air, and move the players back and toss the ball higher as they become accustomed to using their gloves. Using a fungo here is a waste of time, as nobody can hit the ball into the sun often enough to make the time spent worthwhile. A machine is the best way to go after your arm blows out (you'll find that your arm probably is in the best shape ever if you're coaching on an everyday basis).

Drill 3—Balls in the Gaps

Players must understand the concept of catching or cutting the ball off in the gaps before they will be able to do the drill and get something out of it.

Line up your outfielders in groups of no more than three—one in center and one in left (if necessary, line up three groups). Begin by rolling the ball into the gap and checking to see if one outfielder is taking the short angle and the other the deep angle. Explain that the centerfielder goes for the short angle most of the time. Gradually hit the ball harder and mix in fly balls and line drives. Make some of the balls go through so the outfielder must run the ball down and throw to the cutoff man. Remember, the centerfielder is the dominant outfielder, but many times the left-fielder or the rightfielder must be aggressive and take the short angle when the ball is closer to them.

Outfielders must learn to dive for balls in the gaps and toward the lines. The outfielder taking the short angle can dive for the ball with confidence when he knows the other outfielder is taking the deep angle and backing him up. Remember: it is never a good idea to dive for a ball straight ahead—sliding is a much better idea.

Young outfielders often will run to the same place, look at each other, and let the ball roll to the wall. Be patient and realize that without lots of practice and attention to this much-overlooked skill, your outfielders will not execute it properly.

Drill 4—Ground Balls into the Corners

Most baseball coaches don't spend enough time with their outfielders. At least twice a week coaches should work with their outfielders on throwing.

Put all the outfielders into their positions and place infielders at second base and third base; catchers should be at home plate. Hit grounders to the left-field corner, to the right-field corner, and to the gaps. Alternating corners allows the outfielders to return to their true positions and makes the drill more realistic. You also can put an entire infield in place and hit the ball to the wall occasionally to provide work on cutoffs and relays (if you involve the entire team, be sure to put a pitcher on the mound to back up the bases). Have the outfielders throw the ball to second, third, and home and emphasize hitting the cutoff man and keeping the ball low. Remind them that a throw with a low trajectory freezes the runners and prevents them from taking an extra base.

Each outfielder should make between 15 and 20 throws. This drill will take close to 30 minutes and has many possibilities—you can even have the pitchers run the bases for their conditioning.

6
BASERUNNING

Baserunning has always been an underrated part of baseball. More games are won and lost on baserunning than most people might think. Most players are not aggressive enough on the basepaths because either they don't know what to do or they're afraid to fail—or both. A good baseball coach should never be critical of aggressive baserunners who are thrown out trying to take an extra base. Good baserunning requires good judgment, and players who take their baserunning seriously are usually the best judges of these situations.

Good baserunners

- are aggressive
- always know the game situation
- watch the other team to pick up tendencies
- know their limitations
- think one base ahead
- think of the team first

RUNNING THE BASES

Making Turns

When running to first, the baserunner should concentrate on the bag and run *through* the base—jumping on the last step not only is slower but can result in injury.

As soon as the runner knows that the ball is through the infield and a turn is in order, he should head directly for his "spot." This spot varies from runner to runner and base to base. At first base, the spot is usually about five feet to the right of the bag. As he approaches the spot, he should lean toward the bag and touch it on the inside corner with whichever foot comes up in stride. The technique is the same for the turn at second, but the spot is a few feet closer to the bag. Runners should make aggressive turns—this will pressure the outfielders and force them to make mistakes.

The Primary Lead

When the runner arrives at first, his thoughts should be on the game situation. He should look at the coach for signs and check the defensive positioning. He should think about the pitcher's pickoff move and the catcher's throwing ability.

Ten questions to ask yourself before you take a lead:

1. How many outs are there?
2. Are there other runners on base?
3. What is the score?
4. What does my run represent?
5. Where are the outfielders and infielders playing?
6. What is the pitcher's pickoff move like?
7. Does the catcher have a strong arm, and does he like pickoffs?
8. Does the defense have any special plays?
9. Where is the next hitter likely to hit the ball?
10. Is the coach giving me a sign?

While watching the pitcher and only the pitcher, the runner can assume his primary lead—that is, a premeasured number of steps that he should be able to take safely. He should never jump

6-1. With a maximum lead, the baserunner should go back in to the base headfirst. Note that his head is turned to the outfield side.

or get his feet crossed while taking his lead. The average lead at first is three or four steps (eight feet or so).

If the runner has a substantial lead and a pickoff attempt is made, he will probably go in headfirst (fig. 6-1). He should touch the bag with his right hand on the back edge of the bag. If the runner goes back in standing up, he should use the crossover step: move his right foot first and cross over, take a step with the left foot, and go back into the bag with the right foot (fig. 6-2)—this

6-2. Touching the bag with the right foot is a three-step move.

6-3. Getting back to the bag with the left foot requires only two steps. This is the recommended method.

move takes three steps. I recommend crossing over and going into the bag with the left foot (fig. 6-3)—if the runner can't reach the bag with two steps, he should be diving in anyway.

The Secondary Lead

When the pitch is thrown, the runner must gain some ground and assume his secondary lead. Some players are satisfied with taking a little step or two and watching the ball approach the plate. But a good baserunner takes an aggressive secondary lead on every pitch: a crossover step (fig. 6-4) and then a hop (fig. 6-5), coming down on the right foot as the ball is crossing the hitting area (fig. 6-6). If his timing is right, the runner will be able to come down on the right foot, cross over, and never lose momentum toward the base if the ball is hit. This timing will only be developed through lots of practice on the bases.

The Lead at Second

The job of the runner who reaches second base is to score runs. He cannot let the infielders disturb him—if they force him back to

6-4, 6-5, and 6-6. For a secondary lead (with the ball on its way to the plate), the runner should use a crossover step and a hop, and he should land on his right foot as the ball is crossing the hitting area.

second, he may miss a scoring opportunity. His lead can be best described as a "safe maximum" lead: the greatest possible distance without running a risk of being picked off. The length of this lead is determined by the runner's quickness, the pitcher's move, and the importance of the potential run. The "safe maximum" lead makes it unnecessary for the third base coach to give voice commands.

The Lead at Third

The lead at third is a "walking lead." The runner should begin at about the same distance from third as that of the third baseman. He should then walk two or three steps down the line in foul territory, landing on the right foot as the ball crosses the hitting area (fig. 6-7). The manager may elect to send the runner on contact: to break toward the plate on any ball hit. He can be doubled off on some balls, but this is a chance the coach or manager takes.

On a squeeze play, the runner must wait for the pitcher's arm to start forward (when his stride foot hits) before breaking for the

6-7. At third, the runner should take a walking lead and land on his right foot as the ball reaches the hitting area.

plate. If the hitter misses the sign or the ball, the runner should try to stay in the rundown until the other baserunners can move up (this is a good idea any time a runner is trapped between bases).

Runners on all the bases should tag up—even on fly balls in foul territory with less than two outs—and advance whenever possible. It's important to know the strength of the outfielder's arm and to watch his body position just as he catches the ball—it is easy to advance if a player catches the ball in poor position to throw.

Getting a Jump

For a potential basestealer, an 8-to-10-foot lead is not good enough. He must get a bigger primary lead than the average runner, and he must assume this lead whether he is going or not. When he breaks, he should pivot on his right foot (fig. 6-8) and take the first step with his left foot (fig. 6-9). *During the first few steps it's very important that the basestealer stays low*—if he pops up as soon as he starts (fig. 6-10), he will lose balance, direction, and timing.

6-8 and 6-9. To break on a steal or hit-and-run, the runner should pivot on his right foot and take a crossover step. He should remember to stay low as he breaks.

6-10. When a runner pops up he loses time and speed.

6-11. The basestealer should watch the front shoulder of the right-handed pitcher: it will open toward first when he throws to first and close when he throws to home.

If the pitcher's unloading time is slower than 1.3 seconds, he should be easy to steal on. Right-handers who are 1.5 seconds or more are almost automatics; the pitcher who gets to 1.1 or 1.2 seconds is very hard to steal on, even for those with success rates of over 80 percent.

Most pitchers have certain characteristics that indicate whether they are going to first or to the plate. The two areas that major leaguers watch are the front shoulder and the left knee. The pitcher has to lift his front leg and close his front shoulder to deliver the ball to the plate; in order to come to first, he must open the shoulder toward first base. I recommend that young players watch only the left shoulder of the right-handed pitcher (fig. 6-11).

I have found that left-handed pitchers are either very easy or very tough to steal on. Some left-handers lift their hands higher when they come to first (fig. 6-12) than when they go home (fig. 6-13). Some open their right leg when going to first (fig. 6-14) and

6-12 and 6-13. Some left-handed pitchers lift their hands high when going to first and leave them at the belt to go home (or vice versa).

6-14 and 6-15. Other left-handers will open their right leg when going to first and close off the leg when going to home.

close it when going to the plate (fig. 6-15). When they close off this far and break the plane of the rubber they must go to the plate. (A pitcher can't throw to first base if the front foot breaks the plane of the rubber.) With just two umpires at some levels, this is a tough call to get. Other left-handers look at home (fig. 6-16) and throw to first and look to first and throw to home (fig. 6-17).

When a left-handed pitcher is so tough that the baserunner can't get a jump at all, I recommend getting a short lead (enticing him to go home) and breaking on the first move he makes. Some left-handers try to "hang" and watch the runner. Even if the pitcher throws to first and the runner has broken on his first move, the runner will still beat some of these plays at second, especially with a right-handed first baseman.

THE STEAL AND THE HIT-AND-RUN

From the baserunner's view, the differences between the steal and hit-and-run are minimal; the biggest one involves the jump. *When*

6-16 and 6-17. Still other left-handers will look to home and throw to first or look to first and throw to home.

the steal is on, the baserunner is trying to get the perfect jump. If he doesn't get it, he should abort the steal. It is advisable to look in on the third or fourth step to see the ball crossing the hitting zone—it shouldn't slow down a runner to glance in for an instant, and it may save him from getting doubled off on short fly balls. He should not look at the infielders when stealing, as they may try to decoy him by pretending to field a ground ball when the ball has been hit in the air.

When the hit-and-run is on, the baserunner is not looking for that great jump and therefore can't get picked off under any circumstances. *If the runner doesn't get a good jump on a hit-and-run he must go anyway*—the hitter is trying to put the ball in play and stay out of the double play. As in an attempted steal, the runner must look in on the third or fourth step to see the ball crossing the hitting area. This timing can be developed only in batting practice in a live situation with concentration and hard work.

EFFECTIVE AND SAFE SLIDING TECHNIQUES

One of the first things that a youth league coach should teach kids is to slide. At the San Diego School of Baseball players must be able to slide properly in order to play in games. The potential for injury due to improper sliding technique is great.

When learning to slide, players first must practice on grass and without shoes. Sliding is fun, and players at all levels like to work on it. In spring training at major and minor league camps we wet down the grass, take the shoes off, and even 35-year-old superstars have a blast sliding around.

The straight bent-leg slide is the only slide players ever have to learn. It is advisable, but not mandatory, that players learn to slide on both sides. Here are some important things to remember about sliding:

- On any close play, or when in doubt, slide.
- Never slow down or be tentative—slide hard.
- Slide early—never late.
- Go straight into the bag to the area you have committed to—runners get hurt trying to avoid tags.
- Never put one hand down to brace yourself.
- Your lead leg should touch the bag.
- Never slide headfirst into home plate.

When the player puts his hand down (fig. 6-18), he is not only risking a wrist injury; he also tends to turn his body, causing him to hit the ground on his hip bone. (And, as every player will attest, the resulting "strawberry" is very painful.) He must keep his hands up at all times during the slide—this forces him to go straight in, hit on his calf, and slide on his buttocks (fig. 6-19).

The sliding baserunner must break up the double play aggressively, safely, and legally. The rules state that the runner must slide so that he can touch the base with a normal effort (this varies somewhat from league to league). The shortstop usually comes across the bag and throws from the right-field side of second (fig. 6-20); the second baseman, from the left-field side (fig. 6-21). The runner should slide directly into the path (feet first—never headfirst) of the middle infielder, aiming for his left foot to disrupt his ability to complete the throw.

6-18. When a player sliding puts his hand down, he is looking for a sprained wrist or a big strawberry on his hip.

6-19. Most sliding injuries can be avoided by keeping the hands in the air.

6-20 and 6-21. When the shortstop is turning the double play, the baserunner should slide to the right-field side of second to break up the double play. If the second baseman is turning it, he should slide to the left-field side.

AGGRESSIVE BASERUNNING

Baserunning is a fun part of the game a player can practice on his own. *If every player on the team wins one game over the course of the season with good aggressive baserunning, the team can go from last place to first place.* The one area all fans can relate to is the effort that a player puts forth on the bases. If a player wants to sell himself and his attitude to fans and coaches, the bases are the place to do it.

COACHES' CORNER: BASERUNNING AND SLIDING DRILLS

Drill 1—The Hit-and-Run Drill

Every coach would like to have a team with great pitching and defense and an offense that would keep the three-run homers flying out of the ballpark. Unfortunately, it usually doesn't work out that way. Most coaches have to try to manufacture runs any way they can. This usually requires that players have the ability to execute the hit-and-run and, if you are blessed with the speed, to steal bases.

Set up a defensive team on the field (or just an infield) and put at least six runners at first base and at least four hitters in a hitting group. Throw batting practice to the group. Each hitter tries to hit the ball on the ground as the runner at first goes on the hit-and-run. The runners should practice looking in on the second or third step and reacting to the ball off the bat (if the ball is popped up, they should slam on the brakes and go back; on line drives they should keep going—they will be out anyway). Most players simply go through the motions in batting practice, so this drill can be very beneficial. The pitcher should throw to first base once in a while to keep the baserunners honest (a runner should never get picked off on a hit-and-run play because he should not be looking for a stealing jump). The drill usually lasts about 20 minutes, but I like to make a contest out of it: the hitters and baserunners and the defense can take turns to see how many successful hit-and-runs they can do during the drill.

Drill 2—Scoring Position Drill

Set up a defense and put at least three runners at second and at least three runners at home. As you hit fungo base hits to the outfield, the runners at second try to score. It is important that you have a pitcher on the mound holding the runner at second to make the timing of this drill realistic. You also need a third-base coach. The player who starts at the plate should read the flight of the incoming throw and try to advance to scoring position (second) if possible. The job of the defense is to throw the runner out at home and at the very least not let another man advance to scoring position. The outfielders can work on their throws to the plate, the infielders can work on cutoffs and relays, and the catcher can practice tagging. It is not a good idea to run this drill 100 percent live: someone could get hurt running into the catcher.

The runners should rotate until everyone has four or five opportunities to score; then the defense can switch in and out so everyone gets a chance to score on the play. The drill should last no more than 20 minutes.

Drill 3—Basestealing Drill

Players can steal bases with just average speed if they learn to get great jumps. Put your most promising potential basestealers at first base and position a first baseman and middle infielder to catch the throws and make the tags at second. You will also need at least one right-handed pitcher, one left-handed pitcher (why not work on pickoffs with your pitchers at the same time?), and catchers to throw through on the steal attempts.

The runners should work for their leads and try to get a good jump off the pitcher. For best results, have a "green light" sign on instead of a "must go"; in other words, let the runner get a jump and go whenever he wishes instead of making him go on every pitch. This drill should go no more than 15 minutes.

You also may use this drill to practice stealing third and the double steal with runners on first and third or first and second. This drill has lots of possibilities. Remember—don't blow out your catchers' arms. A catcher should make more than 20 to 25 throws a day no more than three times a week in a practice situation.

Drill 4—"Get them over from second" Drill

Players must understand how important it is to move a runner from second to third with no outs. Hitting the ball to the right side is a very important part of every team's offense. This drill can be done with a complete infield defense and runners at second with the coach hitting the fungo or with the coach or someone else throwing batting practice and a group of hitters trying to hit the ball on the ground to the right side of the diamond. The outfielders can begin as the baserunners at second. It is a good idea to have a third-base coach.

The runners should line up one at a time at second and read the ball as it is hit, advancing when it is appropriate to do so. *The old rule "make the ball be through in front of you" is not necessarily true:* a runner with the proper secondary lead and jump may be able to advance to third on a slow-hit ball that pulls the third baseman from his normal position. The runner on second should always know where the third baseman and shortstop are playing. A ball hit sharply in the hole will always get through when the shortstop is playing straight away. Encourage runners to try to stretch the limits of good judgments and be super-aggressive during drills. It is a good opportunity for a player to find out that he can do something he didn't think he was capable of doing.

This drill should last from 15 to 30 minutes depending on whether hitters or a fungo is used.

Drill 5—"Score the runner from third" Drill

Place runners at third base one at a time. The infield should be playing in to cut off the run. As a hitter (or a fungo by the coach) puts the ball in play, the runner should react to the ball—either go on contact or make the ball be through. He also should be alert for wild pitches and can tag up on fly balls to the outfield.

This drill not only helps the runners improve their judgment but also helps the infielders with their skills and can help the hitter improve his execution (if hitters are used in the drill). This drill will last about 15 to 20 minutes and moves very quickly, especially if the fungo is used.

Drill 6—Team Sliding Drill

The most fun I ever have as a coach is with team sliding drills—everyone loves to slide. This drill should be done before your team's first game. Have the players take off their shoes and slide on the grass; wetting it slightly makes this drill even safer. The base should not be tied down—if you don't have flat bases, a towel will do.

You also may take it a step further and have some of the players tag runners as they slide in. When the runner gets 15 feet or so from the base, toss a ball (a soft version of a baseball is best for this drill) to the tagger and let him practice making tags. Since you are throwing the ball to the tagger, you can make the plays as close as you like. Everyone has fun with this drill.

7
HITTING

BATS AND GRIPS

Most young hitters try to use bats that are too big. Parents typically will buy their child a big new aluminum bat for Christmas and figure the young hitter will grow into it. The only problem is that the hitter hits .150 while he's waiting to grow. In professional baseball, where only wood bats are used, the problem of the heavy bat is even more prevalent. A heavy bat can cause a variety of mechanical mistakes: poor bat speed, lack of overall balance, less than clear vision, and a poor path for the bat head. Defects in a hitter's swing may develop that are very difficult to correct at a later date.

Much has been said and written about the grip—people say to line up this knuckle or that finger. But the truth is everyone is different. The bat should be held out in the fingers rather than back in the palm, but the knuckles of different hitters line up differently. The hitter should let the handle of the bat rest against the base of his fingers (fig. 7-1). When the bat is centered and feels comfortable, he should simply close his hands (fig. 7-2).

The firmness of the grip is also an important factor. Veteran hitting instructor Bob Skinner likened it to holding a live bird without crushing him or letting him get away. Hitters will automatically firm up their grip as the bat approaches the impact area.

Why hitters should not use a heavy bat:

- It is difficult to control and causes a hitter to strike out more.
- It forces the hitter to pull out his front side and use more upper body to swing.
- It can slow bat speed and cause a loss of power.
- It can cause permanent mechanical damage.

It is worth noting that perennial National League batting champion Tony Gwynn uses the lightest bat in the major leagues.

7-1. To attain the proper grip, place the bat at the base of your fingers.

7-2. The alignment of the knuckles is an individual matter; all hands—and therefore all grips—are different.

7-3. The open stance is not recommended for most hitters.

STANCES

There are three basic hitting stances: open (fig. 7-3), straightaway (fig. 7-4), and closed (fig. 7-5). You can see many variations of these in the major leagues, but by far the most popular and most effective is the slightly closed stance. My favorite hitter, Tony Gwynn, uses this stance. It allows for good plate coverage, clear vision, and freedom to clear the hips to the ball. Tony and I recommend the slightly closed stance to our students at the San Diego School of Baseball.

Although you hit from the position that you are in after the stride, it is still a good idea to check for plate coverage in your initial position (fig. 7-6). I see many young hitters who stand too close to the plate in their initial stance. When they stride at the pitcher as they should, the good part of the bat is out over the outside corner of the plate, and the handle is over the heart of the plate (fig. 7-7).

7-4. The straightaway stance is used by most major leaguers.

7-5. The slightly closed stance is very popular with big-league hitters.

7-6. To check for plate coverage, simply place the bat across the plate with a normal effort.

7-7. This stance is too close to the plate: the bat handle is over the heart of the plate and the barrel of the bat is over the outside corner.

Hitters from major leaguers to Little Leaguers should not be too concerned with the stance. There are great hitters who hold their hands high, others low, some close to their bodies, others far away. It really doesn't matter where the hands are. A hitter should get comfortable, make sure that he has plate coverage, and forget about his hands.

GETTING THE BAT TO THE BALL

Before the hitter begins his swing, he prepares for the swing with a cocking action of the bat. This "trigger" is an attempt to overcome the dead weight, or inertia, of the bat. In simple terms, it is easier to swing the bat forward if you first put the bat in motion.

Many hitting coaches think that a hitch is a bad thing and should be eliminated. But to hitters the movement functions as a timing device—altering it in any way could destroy their natural timing. *As long as the hands return to a hitting position (the area just below the shoulder), don't worry about a hitch.* Among the many well-known hitters with a pronounced hitch are Hank Aaron, Babe Ruth, Dave Winfield, and Steve Garvey.

The hands must not drift forward during the stride. They must remain back in the hitting position until the stride foot is down. As the hands begin their route to the ball, they will pass close to the body and extend out from there, actually leading the bat head toward the ball for a few inches.

When the bat starts forward, the bottom hand must drive the knob of the bat down (fig. 7-8) in order to bring the bat head down and begin the correct path to the ball. If the bottom hand rides up (fig. 7-9), this initiates a terrible chain of events that makes a level swing impossible. This incorrect path with the bottom hand is called a "chicken wing." *The hands must put the head of the bat on the path of the ball as soon as possible and keep it there as long as possible. This is what is called the "inside-out swing" and is the most efficient way to hit a baseball.*

Tony Gwynn and Wade Boggs are two examples of hitters who use the inside-out swing. Successful hitters get the bat head on the plane of the ball early and maintain that plane longer (using good extension), thus increasing their margin for error. If

7-8. A hitter should drive the knob of the bat (bottom hand) down in order to obtain a level swing.

7-9. When a hitter lets the bottom hand come up, it is called a chicken wing and will not give him good results.

a hitter uppercuts, his bat head is first below the hitting plane, on it for a short time, and then above it. If he hits down on the ball too much, he will be above the ball, on it briefly, and then below it. The idea of extending the hitting plane was for the most part ignored by hitting instructors until the late Charlie Lau (through his student George Brett) made baseball aware of its significance. *The only practical and efficient way to hit a baseball is with a short, quick inside-out swing that allows the bat head to travel for a longer elapsed time on the plane of impact.*

7-10. If the stride is too long, it can inhibit the hips, causing an uppercut swing and loss of balance and weight transfer.

STRIDE AND WEIGHT TRANSFER

The length of the stride has been the subject of much discussion, but in my opinion the length of a hitter's stride is not important. Unless it is ridiculously long and locks up the hips (fig. 7-10), it is nothing to be concerned about. The elapsed time of the stride is almost identical to the elapsed time of the trigger. The two events happen simultaneously and are tied together mechanically— changes in one will affect the other.

The stride should be toward the pitcher or slightly closed, and the foot should be planted at about a 45-degree angle. If the stride toe opens too much (fig. 7-11), the hitter will land on his heel and spin, causing his front side to open, which in turn will impede a complete weight transfer and can hinder the complete opening of the hips. *If the hitter simply steps toward the pitcher and does not try to make the stride a powerful movement, he is on the way to keeping his head still, and good balance is usually the result.*

7-11. If the toe of the stride foot opens, the hitter will experience lots of mechanical problems. This is probably the most common mechanical flaw that Tony Gwynn and I see in young players at the San Diego School of Baseball.

The stride initiates the all-important weight transfer by taking some pressure off the back foot, which allows the hips to begin rotation. After the stride puts the body in motion, the body weight travels forward until it meets resistance from the front leg. The hitter then "blocks" against this firm front leg and creates the leverage necessary to deliver a powerful blow to the ball. Without this blocking effect the hitter can use little of his power, and he will deliver a weak and ineffective blow. This method of gaining leverage is based on the same principle used by pitchers, kickers, boxers, javelin throwers, and others. The stride, weight transfer, hip rotation, and followthrough are all interrelated. A mechanical error in one can adversely affect the next movement of the sequence.

The hitter can prolong the time that the bat head travels toward the ball by reaching out "through" the ball as he hits it. Proper weight transfer naturally extends the range that the bat head can travel forward on the path of the ball. This is the essence of Charlie Lau's approach to hitting.

Preparation
- Weight shifts back toward catcher to trigger body movements that follow.
- Heel of stride foot comes up.
- Eyes focused at 60 feet, switch to release point as pitcher starts forward toward plate.

1st Stage of Swing
- Eyes first pick up ball at release point and begin tracking process.
- Forward stride begins.
- Hands trigger bat.

2nd Stage of Swing
- Hands arrive at hitting position.
- Stride foot is planted.
- Tracking very critical at this stage (decision to swing or not is made during this period).

THE TIMING CHAIN

Preparation

0.00 seconds

1st Stage

0.10 seconds

2nd Stage

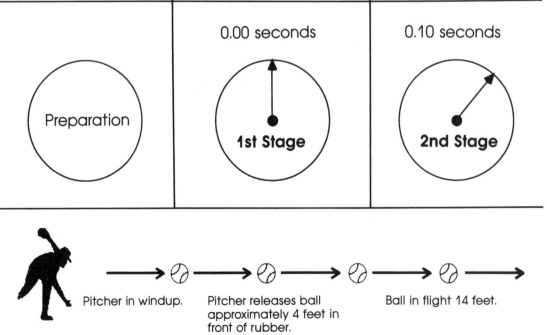

Pitcher in windup.

Pitcher releases ball approximately 4 feet in front of rubber.

Ball in flight 14 feet.

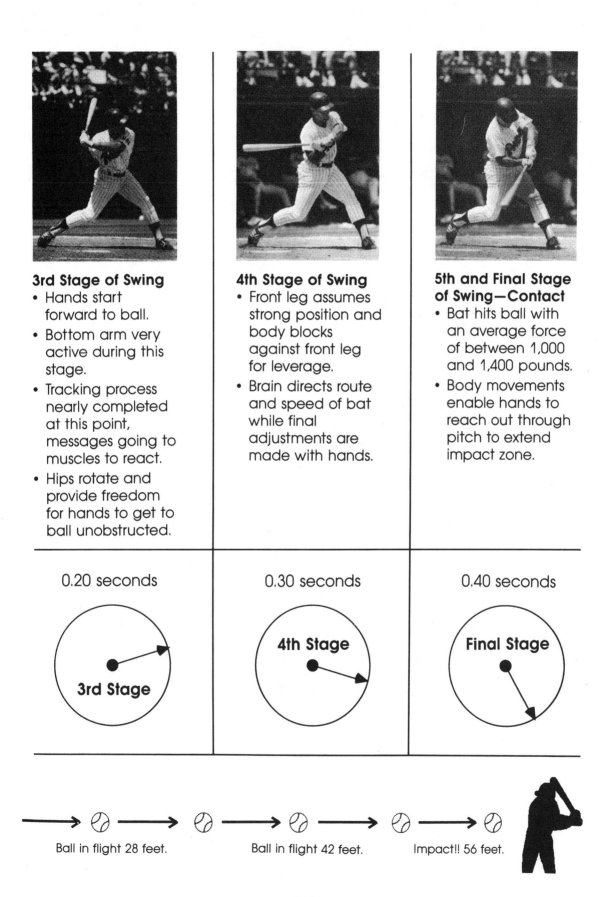

3rd Stage of Swing
- Hands start forward to ball.
- Bottom arm very active during this stage.
- Tracking process nearly completed at this point, messages going to muscles to react.
- Hips rotate and provide freedom for hands to get to ball unobstructed.

4th Stage of Swing
- Front leg assumes strong position and body blocks against front leg for leverage.
- Brain directs route and speed of bat while final adjustments are made with hands.

5th and Final Stage of Swing—Contact
- Bat hits ball with an average force of between 1,000 and 1,400 pounds.
- Body movements enable hands to reach out through pitch to extend impact zone.

0.20 seconds

3rd Stage

0.30 seconds

4th Stage

0.40 seconds

Final Stage

Ball in flight 28 feet.

Ball in flight 42 feet.

Impact!! 56 feet.

171

THE HITTING PROCESS

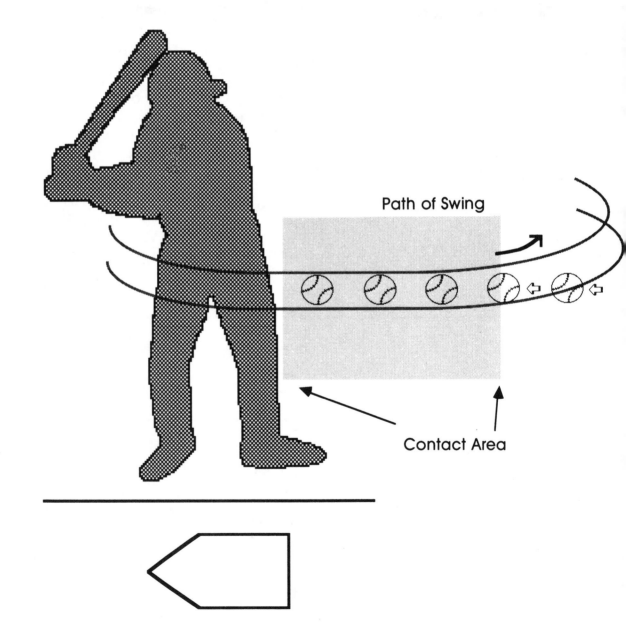

Path of Swing

Contact Area

Flight of Incoming Pitch

TRACKING THE BALL

The most important factor in the success of a hitter is how clearly and for how long he sees the ball. Kids hear clichés like "watch the ball all the way in" or "see the ball hit the bat" from the time they are five or six years old. Even though this is good information, the hitter needs advice that targets the root of the problem, not the symptoms. We need to tell hitters *how* to see the ball more effectively.

Three reasons why hitters don't see the ball clearly:

1. Poor eyesight is always a possibility—every athlete should get his eyes checked on a regular basis.
2. Hitters who try to pull the ball or hit it into the air will often lift their heads and lose focus. This flaw is easily recognized: the chin comes up just before impact.
3. Every hitter that has ever lived has had problems with overswinging. Trying to hit the ball too hard will absolutely destroy mechanics and clear vision.

7-12. A hitter should concentrate on the pitcher's release point and try to get the ball in clear focus as soon as possible.

A hitter must keep his head down from the beginning of the swing until extension is complete. In all athletic movements, the direction and overall balance of the body is dictated by the direction and position of the head. It is no secret that all successful hitters keep their heads still during their swing.

Coaches should begin every practice session by having players hit ground balls up the middle and to the opposite field with easy, controlled swings, keeping their heads as still as possible. During the workout they can swing a little harder, but if the ball fades out or gets fuzzy, they must cut it back once again to the easy swing.

The hitter picks up the ball out of the pitcher's hand at his release point (fig. 7-12). One method that can help the hitter to focus more sharply in a much shorter time is to focus on the pitcher's cap during the windup and then switch to his release point as his arm comes forward. The theory is that the ball will come into focus faster with the eyes already focused at a distance of 60 feet.

Like a built-in computer, the hitter's brain gathers information about each pitch and sends commands to the muscles to move the bat. Information starts to arrive in the brain as soon as the ball gets into focus. Studies indicate that *the direction and trajectory of the pitch are the first bits of information to be processed* (this is very helpful if the pitch is at your helmet). *The information that is most difficult—and therefore takes the most time—for the brain to process involves the speed of the pitch.* (Why do you think change-ups work so well?)

The eyes aren't the only means by which the hitter tracks the ball. The vestibular system of the inner ear (used for balance) tells him where he is in space and therefore where the head of the bat is at all times. The brain puts this information together, computes the timing, and directs the speed and direction of the swing. This entire process happens in less than one-half second.

Horizontally speaking, a four-inch-wide area called the center of percussion, the "sweet spot" (fig. 7-13), is the most effective part of the bat with which to hit the ball. Vertically speaking, an error of as little as an eighth of an inch in a swing can result in a fly ball instead of a line drive. And what's worse, the timing has to be almost perfect to hit the ball hard. When the baseball reaches the impact area, it remains hittable for approximately 48

7-13. The center of percussion—the "sweet spot."

inches of its flight—to put the ball in fair territory, only 24 to 30 inches. *A ball thrown at 90 miles per hour only remains hittable in fair territory for a time estimated at .015 (fifteen thousandths) of a second.* Theoretically, if a swing starts .02 (two hundredths) of a second too early or too late, the hitter will miss the ball. *This is why it is so important to keep the head still in order to see the ball clearly.*

BUNTING

There are two basic styles for sacrifice bunting. The pivot method is so called because the hitter pivots on his back foot to rotate and face the pitcher. The only real disadvantage of this method is the impaired ability to bunt the outside pitch. The square-around method calls for the bunter to bring his back foot around to face the pitcher and positions it slightly ahead of the lead foot. This style provides for more flexibility and makes it easier to reach more pitches with less effort. Most big leaguers as well as veteran instructor Bunny Mick, "The Bunting Guru," recommend squaring around. The following fundamentals apply to both methods.

When the batter assumes the bunting position, he should hold the bat level and at the top of the strike zone and flex his legs slightly (fig. 7-14) so that he will be prepared to bend when the ball is down in the strike zone (fig. 7-15). The direction of the bunt is predetermined—if the angle remains constant until ball meets bat, the ball must go in the desired direction. With a runner on first and less than two outs, the ball must be bunted down the first-base line; with a runner on second, the ball must be bunted toward third base.

7-14. The bunter should keep the bat level at the top of the strike zone and the legs flexed.

7-15. As the bunter goes down after the low pitch, he will bend with his legs and not with his back.

In order to make the ball stop in a specific area, the bunter must pull the bat back with *both* hands as contact is made. If he pulls with one more than the other, the angle will be changed. Another method of killing the ball is to bunt it on the extreme end of the bat.

When bunting for a base hit, the hitter must decide where he will bunt the ball and stick to the plan. His decision will be largely influenced by the positioning of the infielders and the pitcher's fielding abilities. Bunting for a base hit involves the same mechanics as the sacrifice bunt; the major differences are that the hitter needs to disguise this bunt as long as possible, and he must gain some momentum toward first base.

When bunting the ball to third, the batter can use a drop step with his back foot (fig. 7-16), or he can take a step with his front foot (fig. 7-17). If he is attempting a push bunt toward second base, he should step with his right foot toward the second-base position (fig. 7-18). Left-handed bunters should step toward the pitcher with the left foot on bunts to both areas (fig. 7-19 and fig. 7-20).

7-16. One method of bunting for a base hit to third is the drop step.

7-17. Another way to bunt to third is to move the front foot forward.

7-18. To "push bunt" toward second, most big leaguers move the left foot and push the ball toward the second baseman's position.

7-19 and 7-20. The left-handed bunter can move his left foot forward and bunt to third or first by changing the angle of the bat (the bunt toward the second-base position must be firmer to get by the pitcher).

Remember—the bunter must get a good pitch. If the pitch is not a strike or is not a good pitch to bunt, then he should abort the bunt, pull the bat back, and take the pitch.

Even if the batter just shows a bunt periodically, this will still bring the defense in and give him an advantage when he swings away.

SITUATIONAL HITTING

Hitters must learn to respond properly to various game situations. Coaches should demand that their players practice these hitting situations and execute them in games.

Man on second—no outs or one out

The objective here is to hit the ball to the right side of the diamond on the ground to get the runner to third with one out or less. Once you get two strikes, protect the plate and just make contact. Hitting balls off a batting tee placed in different areas will help develop this skill.

The hit-and-run

The hit-and-run play requires the batter to hit the ball anywhere on the ground. This is a skill that a hitter should develop by the high school level. Driving the bottom hand down will help to hit the ball on the ground.

Man on third and less than two outs—infield back

It sounds easy, but hitting a ground ball to first base, second base, or shortstop is not always that easy. The defense is giving a free run, but some hitters have trouble driving it in. Those who do should work with a batting tee, focusing on driving down on the bottom hand.

Tying run at the plate—two outs, late in the game

The hitter's job here is to try for an extra-base hit; if he is not a basestealing threat, then there is no other alternative. The key is to be patient and wait for a pitch to drive. This doesn't mean an all-out wild swing, but an aggressive approach to this at bat is necessary.

COACHES' CORNER: SOLVING HITTING PROBLEMS

Every hitting instructor must develop his own program and his own approach to solving problems. *The key is to work on the root of the problem, not the symptoms, and to avoid creating new problems as you solve old ones.* My hitting program is much like my pitching program in that it is simple and involves lots of time spent on balance and direction. But you can't solve hitting problems unless you and your students are talking the same hitting language. So before you jump into this troubleshooting section, familiarize yourself with the contents of this chapter and make sure your players have a basic understanding of hitting mechanics and terminology.

Problem 1

"Some of my hitters are striking out too much."

Solution

This is usually just a problem of overswinging, but there are some other possibilities.

The first thing that I would consider is the possibility of poor eyesight. If a player displays balance problems after the swing, then you can bet that he is just swinging too hard. If he is overswinging, then he is probably pulling off the ball with his head and front shoulder. Set up a batting tee on the outside corner of the plate (fig. 7-21) and have him hit 50–100 balls a day up the middle on the ground. Emphasize to him that he should hit the ball hard on the ground and keep the ball out of the air. I would also check the player's bat—a bat that is too heavy will cause him to use too much upper body out of necessity.

Hitters must develop a two-strike approach in order to guard against the strikeout. The adjustment can be as simple as choking up an inch or two on the bat and cutting down on the swing. Some hitters spread out their stance three or four inches, and some even

7-21. By using the batting tee with the ball placed on the outside corner, the player is forced to go to the ball and is unable to pull off the ball and step away.

eliminate their strides altogether. Another effective method can be to try to hit the ball back through the middle, or, as they say, "gap to gap."

Problem 2

"One of my hitters has a bad uppercut."

Solution

Not an easy problem to fix—a total overhaul is necessary.

Most kids use a heavy bat during their early years, which leads directly to an uppercut. In Tee Ball, the adults place the tee too close to the batter, and the fielders are so close that the natural instinct of the hitter is to hit the ball over their heads. Every kid wants to be a hero, to go for the big one. In severe cases the hips don't open, there is no weight transfer, and the kid falls around after the swing with very little balance. If you have a hitter who can't touch the ball above the waist but really hits the low ball well, you've got a classic uppercutter on your hands.

To correct this problem you must change the toughest computer program of all, the muscle memory of the human brain. And the job becomes more difficult as the player's career progresses.

7-22. By placing the tee on a box, you can make the ball at least letter high.

Set the batting tee as high in the strike zone as possible—put it up on a box if necessary (fig. 7-22). The ball should be letter high as the hitter stands up to the plate. Have the player hit down on the ball—100, 200 times a day, the more the better.

One of the keys in correcting this problem is changing the path of the bottom hand. The uppercutter has a potentially terminal (as a hitter) disease called the chicken wing (fig. 7-23). When the bottom hand rides up instead of driving down (fig. 7-24), an uppercut is inevitable. Whenever a hitter overswings, the bottom arm takes a more active role in the swing and tries to control the bat. *In order to retrain the bottom arm, you must first isolate the bottom arm on the bat.* Using a bat that is much smaller than the game bat, the player should swing with just his bottom hand (fig. 7-25). Emphasize hitting the ball down and reaching "through" the ball. The left hand should drive the knob of the bat down. After the player hits with just the bottom hand for a while, let him take a few swings with both hands using his game bat but still concentrating on driving down with his bottom hand. While re-

7-23. A hitter who lets his bottom arm (right arm on a right-handed hitter) ride up during the swing has a mechanical flaw called a chicken wing.

7-24. The path of the bottom hand should be down and through the ball.

7-25. Using only the bottom arm to swing isolates the chicken wing problem. The overall path of the bat and extension can be improved using this drill.

structuring the path of the bottom hand, keep in mind that the barrel of the bat should remain above the hands at all times. Videotape or film might be very useful to show the hitter the importance of this concept. After he has learned to control the problem somewhat (it will never be eliminated), he should continue working on the tee with just the bottom hand at least once a week.

Problem 3

"One of my hitters hits with locked hips and no weight transfer."

7-26. When the body weight is trapped on the back side, the hips are locked up and no weight transfer can take place.

Solution

When the hips don't open, the last place to look for the answer is the hips.

One of the most important aspects of the swing is the weight transfer. All of the movements associated with moving the body forward are linked together. In order to pivot on the back foot and

7-27. Once the pressure is taken off the rear foot, and providing the hands are driving forward to the ball, opening the hips and transferring the body weight should be an automatic response.

open the hips, the weight must be first taken off the back foot—the hips cannot and will not open with the weight on the back foot (fig. 7-26). When the stride begins, some of the pressure is taken off the rear foot (fig. 7-27). If the hands are driving down on the ball, the weight should continue to transfer and the hips will open.

Begin with the tee placed 18–24 inches in front of home plate (fig. 7-28) and have the batter hit down on the ball (fig. 7-29). He should try to reach out through the ball and get full extension on each swing. Swinging at the tee in this position should force the batter to shift his weight off the rear foot and rotate his hips. Make sure he strides smoothly and does not jump to the front foot—the movement should be smooth, with the weight transferring from back to front with no loss of balance. When his weight transfer shows improvement, you can move the tee back to the normal hitting area (fig. 7-30).

Note: Telling a hitter to spin his hips or show his belly button to the pitcher are not effective means of solving this problem. When a hitter is told to rotate his hips he will almost always start spinning off the ball with his front side and create a whole new set of problems.

7-28. With the tee placed well out in front of the plate, the hitter must transfer his weight as he hits down on the ball.

7-29. By reaching down and through the ball, the hitter will get full extension and a complete weight transfer.

7-30. After the hitter has made some progress, the coach can move the tee back to the regular hitting area.

Problem 4

"Some of my hitters are having problems hitting the inside pitch."

Solution

Sometimes the hitter is standing too close to the plate. But this problem usually means the swing is "long."

First of all, most hitters have trouble with the inside pitch. In the major leagues, advance scouts often find that 90 percent of the hitters on a team have a weakness inside.

When a hitter extends his bat too early (fig. 7-31), the bat head takes a long path to the ball. Remember—the bottom hand must drive the knob of the bat down to allow the hands to stay inside the ball (fig. 7-32). This is the inside-out, or short, swing— the bat head travels a much shorter distance to the ball. Hitters with a long swing will have lots of trouble with the inside pitch. The symptoms this kind of hitter displays are much the same as

7-31. When a hitter extends his bat too early, the path of the bat is long and slow, and the best part of the bat is far out over the plate and out of the hitting area.

7-32. The key to hitting the ball with consistency is the inside-out swing used by Tony Gwynn, Wade Boggs, and others.

those of a severe uppercutter. It is no coincidence that uppercutters have the most trouble with pitches up and in.

Coaches should not make a big deal out of the inside pitch. Hitters should develop an inside-out swing and not concern themselves with the ball inside. An excellent thought process is for the hitter to look for the ball away all the time, take a solid stride back to the pitcher, and just react to the ball inside. *If a hitter has to look for the ball inside in order to hit it, he has little chance to become a good hitter.*

Problem 5
"My hitters just can't hit a good curveball or off-speed pitcher."

Solution
Your hitters can't maintain their weight; drills to keep weight back are the solution.

Good curveballs and off-speed pitches probably present the toughest problem for major league hitters. Pitchers with good change-ups and curveballs usually have long, winning careers. The harder a hitter swings, and the more he tries to pull the ball, the more trouble he will have with pitches slower than the fastball.

Curveballs are hard to hit not so much because they curve but because they are off-speed. Most hitters come out of their shoes swinging at fastball speed and can't wait for the curve to get there. The majority of major league fastballs are between 80 and 90 miles per hour, and most curveballs are between 65 and 78 miles per hour, as much as 15 miles per hour slower. This is a very difficult adjustment for hitters who are geared for the fastball.

Hitters should practice "waiting" on the ball. Placing the batting tee on the outside corner and hitting 50–100 balls a day to the opposite field will help hitters learn to maintain their body weight on their back foot longer.

As a general rule, major league hitters never practice hitting anything but fastballs. This has always amazed me. I have thrown batting practice to hundreds of major and minor league hitters, and I've had maybe 10 guys ask for a few breaking balls or change-ups mixed in. They want all fastballs, usually thrown by a coach at 60–70 miles per hour, and they want them all the same speed. Some hitters will even get upset if you change speeds on a pitch by accident. It is sad that so many hitters at that level are more concerned with looking good than improving their skills. They smack batting practice fastballs out of the park and hear the fans go "oooh" and "aaah" and then take an 0-for-4 on breaking balls and change-ups during the game.

A good coach should throw his hitters a few off-speed pitches during every practice session and force them to hit the ball to the opposite field. If hitters need more practice, hitting 50–100 balls to the opposite field off a tee on the outside corner of the plate will help condition them to wait on the ball. Using the two-strike approach mentioned earlier will help a great deal against a pitcher with a good curve or change. With enough work, a team can learn to be better off-speed hitters.

Problem 6

"I have one or two hitters who step away into the bucket on every swing."

Solution

You must change the entire approach of the hitter.

7-33. When a hitter steps away on every pitch, he is usually either afraid of the ball or trying to pull everything.

When a hitter steps away from the ball on every pitch (fig. 7-33), several factors could be involved. The first thing that you always think about is fear. Depending on the age of the player, it can be terminal (in a baseball sense) or just a temporary problem. Kids usually do not make it to the high school level if they are still afraid of the ball.

7-34. The only way to control the problem of stepping away is by using the batting tee. After hitting hundreds of balls to the opposite field, the player will begin to control the problem and develop new habits.

Lots of kids are first exposed to baseball as I was—in the backyard, at about age five, with Dad throwing batting practice. Fathers usually tell their kids two big lies on that first day: Lie number one is "I won't hit you with the ball," and lie number two is "If I do, it won't hurt." Well, Dad probably drilled you in the ribs on about the sixth pitch. When the crying is over, some kids are not too eager to hit again soon. As time goes by, the fear goes away—almost.

I think the main reason for stepping away from the plate is trying to pull the ball. Trying to pull every pitch has probably destroyed more hitters than anything else, especially at the higher levels. When a hitter tries to pull the ball, many bad things happen mechanically: his front side flies open too soon, he doesn't see the ball as clearly, and as if this weren't bad enough, he is probably on his way to a severe uppercut and an ugly, long, ineffective swing.

The solution? You guessed it—back to the batting tee. Place the tee on the outside corner of the plate and make the hitter dive in and hit every ball to the opposite field (fig. 7-34). Somewhere between 200 and 2,000,000 swings taking the correct approach, his problem will be controlled. Note that I said *controlled*, not corrected; every hitter steps away or comes off the ball at times.

8
THE PLAYBOOK

What is the shortstop's defensive assignment on a single to right field with the bases loaded? What does the rightfielder do on an extra-base hit down the left-field line with a runner on first?

Players must be able to respond almost instantaneously to these and many other fielding situations; failure to do so could be very costly. Good defensive teams are aware of the game situation at all times and know their playbook—forward and backward.

A defensive player has four possible assignments when the ball is hit:

- field the ball
- cover a base
- back up a base or another player
- move to a cutoff (relay) position

There is no assignment called "stand and watch"; every defensive player has an important job to do on every play.

The following playbook illustrates and explains defensive assignments for a wide range of hitting situations with varying combinations of baserunners—from a straightforward single to right with the bases empty to a double, possibly a triple, to right center field with the bases loaded. Also covered in detail are pop flies, wild pitches and passed balls, bunts, and rundown plays.

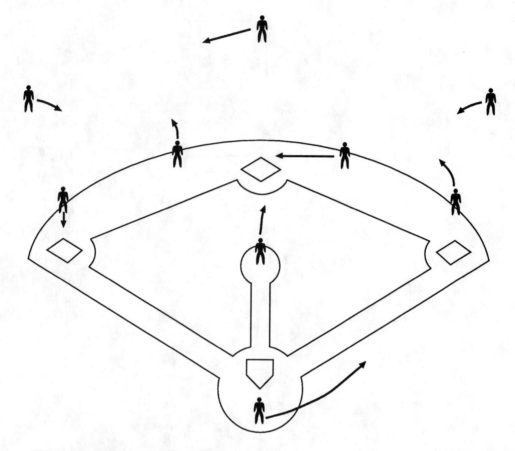

DEFENSIVE ASSIGNMENTS

Single to left field—bases empty

Pitcher: Back up the throw to second base.

Catcher: Cover first base in case the runner makes a wide turn around first.

First baseman: Be sure that the runner touches first base and then back up the incoming throw to second base.

Second baseman: Cover second base.

Shortstop: Go for the ball; then try to line up between the leftfielder and second base and assume the cutoff position.

Third baseman: Cover third base.

Leftfielder: Field the ball and hit the cutoff man (shortstop). If he has been taken out of position attempting to field the ball, then throw the ball directly to second base.

Centerfielder: Back up the leftfielder.

Rightfielder: Move toward infield area in case of a bad throw from the leftfielder to second base.

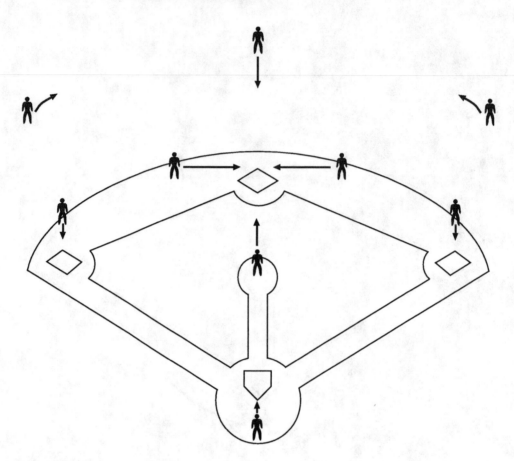

Single to center field—bases empty

Pitcher: Back up the throw to second base.

Catcher: Cover home plate.

First baseman: Be sure that the runner tags first base and then cover the base on the inside.

Second baseman: If the shortstop tries to field the ball, cover second; otherwise, back up the throw to second base.

Shortstop: Cover second base unless you go for the ball and are out of position and can't get back.

Third baseman: Cover third base.

Leftfielder: Back up the centerfielder.

Centerfielder: Field the ball and throw it to second base on one hop.

Rightfielder: Back up the centerfielder.

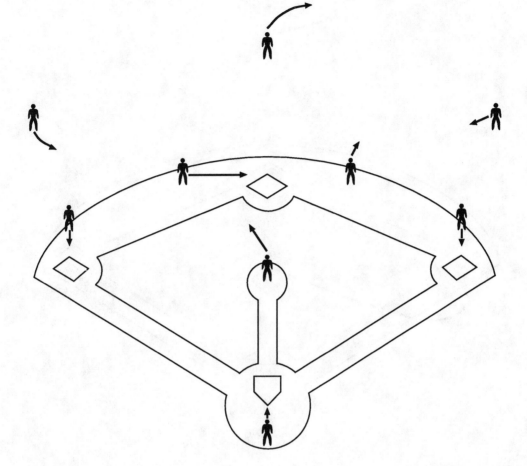

Single to right field—bases empty

Pitcher: Back up the throw to second base.

Catcher: Cover home plate.

First baseman: Be sure that the runner touches first base and then cover the base on the inside. (If you have tried to field the ball, you may be taken out of position.)

Second baseman: Go for the ball; then try to line up between the rightfielder and second base and assume the cutoff position.

Shortstop: Cover second base.

Third baseman: Cover third base.

Leftfielder: Move toward the infield area in case of a bad throw from the rightfielder to second base.

Centerfielder: Back up the rightfielder.

Rightfielder: Field the ball and hit the cutoff man (second baseman). If he has been taken out of position attempting to field the ball, then throw directly to second base.

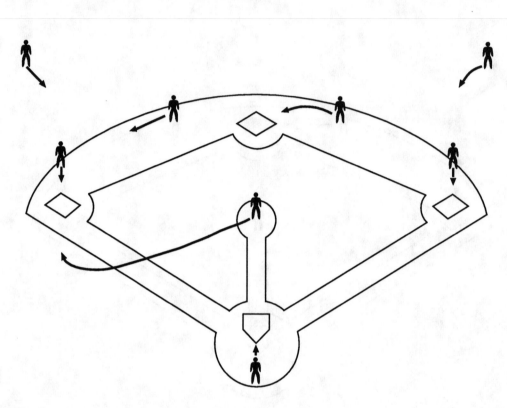

Single to left field—runner on first or runners on first and third

Pitcher: Back up the throw to third base.

Catcher: Cover home plate.

First baseman: Be sure that the runner touches first base and then cover the base on the inside.

Second baseman: Cover second base.

Shortstop: Line up between the leftfielder and third base and assume the cutoff position.

Third baseman: Cover third base.

Leftfielder: Field the ball and hit the cutoff man (shortstop). If he has been taken out of position attempting to field the ball, then throw the ball directly to third base.

Centerfielder: Back up leftfielder.

Rightfielder: Move toward the infield and cover possible overthrows.

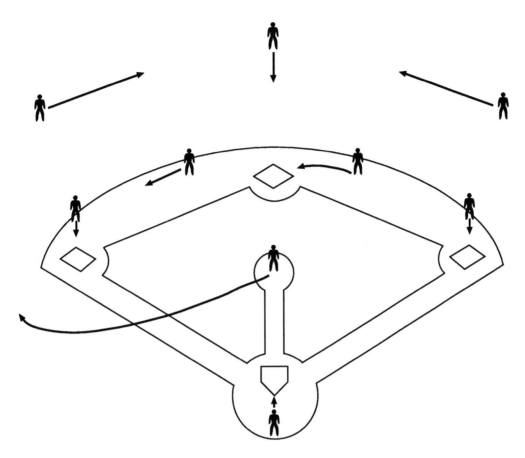

Single to center field—runner on first or runners on first and third

Pitcher: Back up the throw to third base.

Catcher: Cover home plate.

First baseman: Be sure that the runner touches first base and then cover the base on the inside.

Second baseman: Cover second base.

Shortstop: Line up between the centerfielder and third base and assume the cutoff position.

Third baseman: Cover third base.

Leftfielder: Back up the centerfielder.

Centerfielder: Field the ball and hit the cutoff man (shortstop). If he has been taken out of position attempting to field the ball, then throw the ball directly to third base.

Rightfielder: Back up the centerfielder.

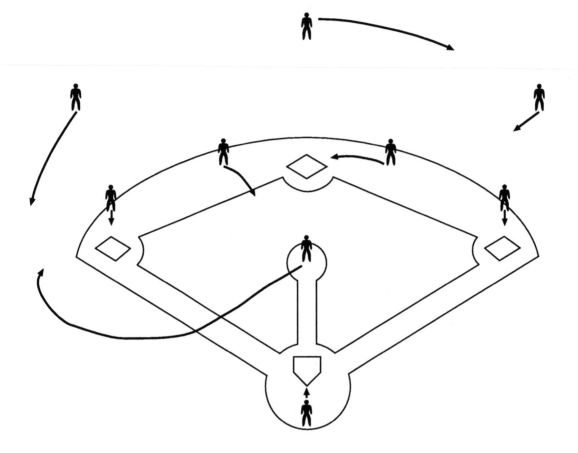

Single to right field—runner on first or runners on first and third

Pitcher: Back up the throw to third base.

Catcher: Cover home plate.

First baseman: Be sure that the runner touches first base and then cover the base on the inside.

Second baseman: Cover second base.

Shortstop: Line up between the rightfielder and third base and assume the cutoff position.

Third baseman: Cover third base.

Leftfielder: Back up the throw to third base.

Centerfielder: Back up the rightfielder.

Rightfielder: Field the ball and hit the cutoff man (shortstop).

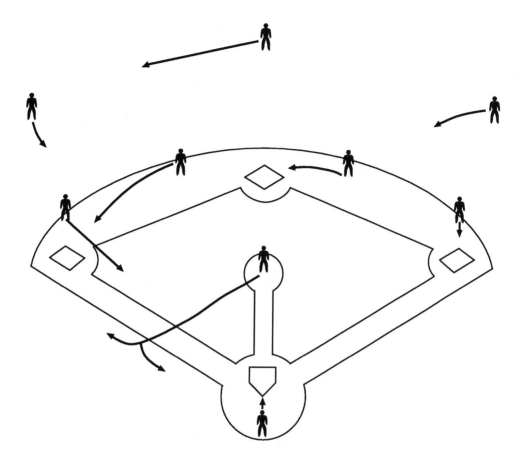

*Single to left field—runner on second, runners on first and second,
or bases loaded*

Pitcher: Go to an area halfway between third base and home plate, read
the play, and back up the throw.

Catcher: Cover home plate.

First baseman: Cover first base.

Second baseman: Cover second base.

Shortstop: Cover third base.

Third baseman: Become the cutoff man for the throw to the plate.

Leftfielder: Field the ball and hit the cutoff man (third baseman).

Centerfielder: Back up the leftfielder.

Rightfielder: Back up throws to the second-base area.

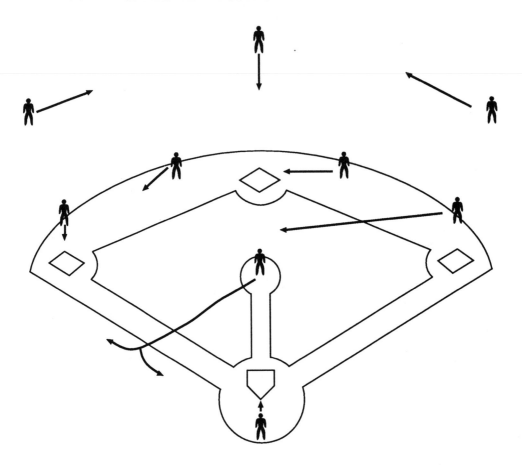

Single to center field—runner on second, runners on first and second, or bases loaded

Pitcher: Go to an area halfway between third base and home plate, read the play, and back up the throw.

Catcher: Cover home plate.

First baseman: Become cutoff man for the throw to the plate.

Second baseman: Cover second base.

Shortstop: Become cutoff man for the throw to third base.

Third baseman: Cover third base.

Leftfielder: Back up the centerfielder and help call the play.

Centerfielder: Field the ball, listen for teammates to call the play, and throw to either the first baseman (the cutoff man for a play at the plate) or the shortstop (the cutoff man for a play at third base).

Rightfielder: Back up the centerfielder and help call the play.

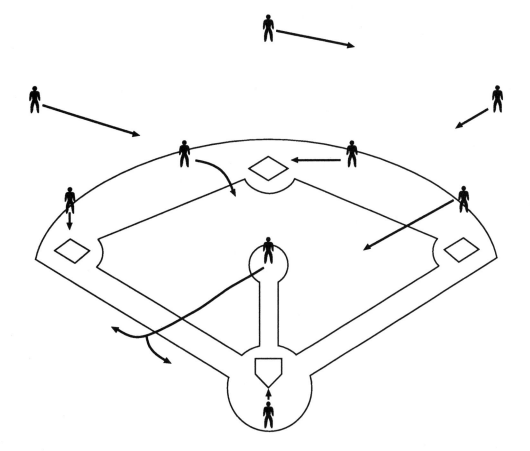

Single to right field—runner on second, runners on first and second, or bases loaded

Pitcher: Go to an area halfway between third base and home plate, read the play, and back up the throw.

Catcher: Cover home plate.

First baseman: Become cutoff man for the throw to the plate.

Second baseman: Cover second base.

Shortstop: Become cutoff man for the throw to third base.

Third baseman: Cover third base.

Leftfielder: Back up throws to the second-base area.

Centerfielder: Back up the rightfielder and help call the play.

Rightfielder: Field the ball, listen for teammates to call the play, and throw to either the first baseman (the cutoff man for a play at the plate) or the shortstop (the cutoff man for a play at third base).

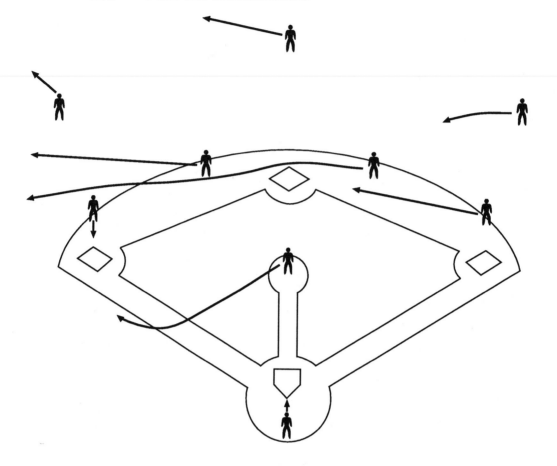

Sure double, possible triple, down the left-field line—bases empty

Pitcher: Back up third base.

Catcher: Cover home plate.

First baseman: Be sure that the runner touches first base and then trail him to second base.

Second baseman: When convinced that the hit is at least a double, assume a trail position 20 feet behind the shortstop.

Shortstop: Assume the cutoff position down the left-field line, in line with third base.

Third baseman: Cover third base.

Leftfielder: Field the ball and hit the cutoff man (shortstop).

Centerfielder: Back up the leftfielder.

Rightfielder: Back up throws to the second-base area.

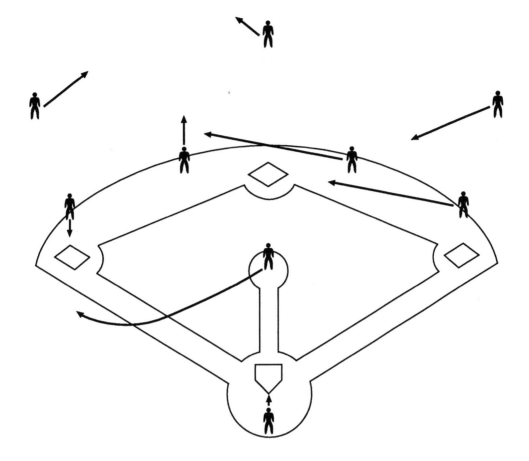

Sure double, possible triple, in the left-center-field gap—bases empty

Pitcher: Back up third base.

Catcher: Cover home plate.

First baseman: Be sure that the runner touches first base and then trail him to second base.

Second baseman: When convinced that the hit is at least a double, assume a trail position 20 feet behind the shortstop.

Shortstop: Assume the cutoff position, in line with third base.

Third baseman: Cover third base.

Leftfielder: Back up the centerfielder.

Centerfielder: Field the ball and hit the cutoff man (shortstop).

Rightfielder: Back up throws to the second-base area.

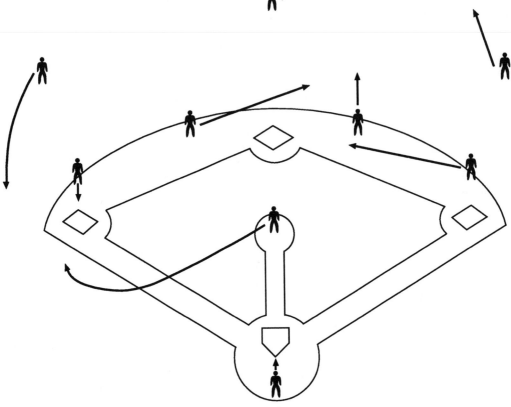

Sure double, possible triple, in the right-center-field gap—bases empty

Pitcher: Back up third base.

Catcher: Cover home plate.

First baseman: Be sure that the runner touches first base and then trail him to second base.

Second baseman: Assume the cutoff position, in line with third base.

Shortstop: When convinced that the hit is at least a double, assume a trail position 20 feet behind the second baseman.

Third baseman: Cover third base.

Leftfielder: Back up the third-base area.

Centerfielder: Field the ball and hit the cutoff man (second baseman).

Rightfielder: Back up the centerfielder.

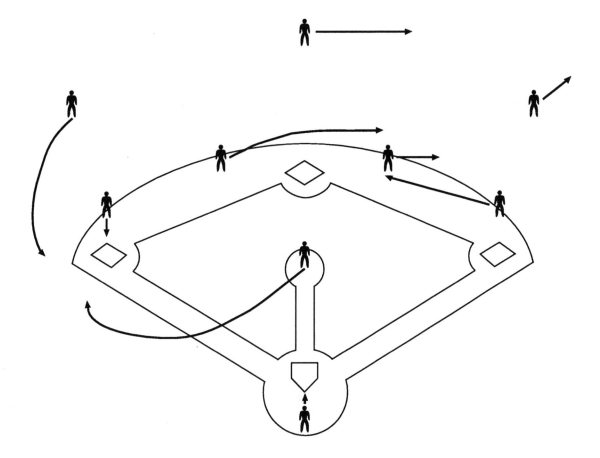

Sure double, possible triple, down the right-field line—bases empty

Pitcher: Back up third base.

Catcher: Cover home plate.

First baseman: Be sure that the runner touches first base and then trail him to second base.

Second baseman: Assume the cutoff position, in line with third base.

Shortstop: When convinced that the hit is at least a double, assume a trail position 20 feet behind the second baseman.

Third baseman: Cover third base.

Leftfielder: Back up the third-base area.

Centerfielder: Back up the rightfielder.

Rightfielder: Field the ball and hit the cutoff man (second baseman).

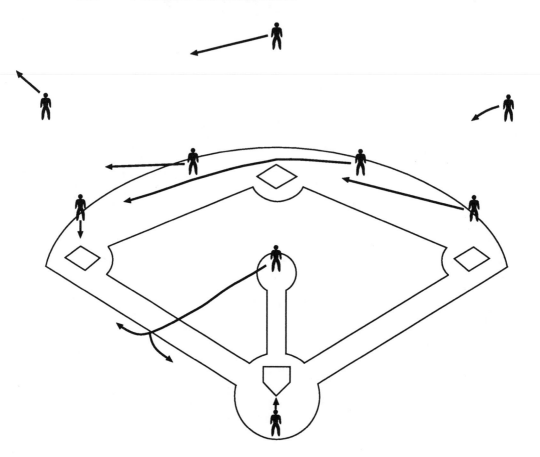

Sure double, possible triple, down the left-field line—men on base

Pitcher: Go to a position halfway between home plate and third base, read the play, and back up the appropriate base.

Catcher: Cover home plate.

First baseman: Be sure that the runner touches first base and then trail him to second base.

Second baseman: When convinced that the hit is at least a double, assume a trail position 20 feet behind the shortstop. Tell the shortstop whether to throw to third or home.

Shortstop: Assume the cutoff position down the left-field line, in line with home plate.

Third baseman: Cover third base.

Leftfielder: Field the ball and hit the cutoff man (shortstop).

Centerfielder: Back up the leftfielder.

Rightfielder: Back up the second-base area.

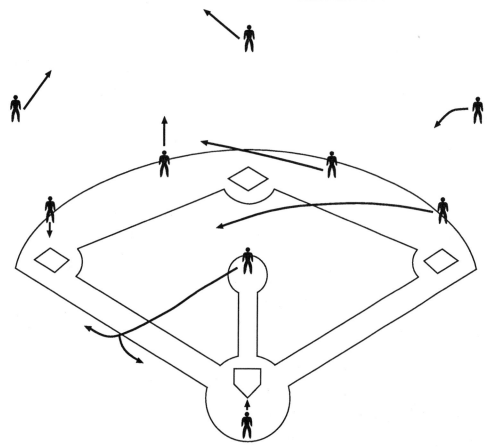

Sure double, possible triple, in the left-center-field gap—men on base

Pitcher: Go to a position halfway between home plate and third base, read the play, and back up the appropriate base.

Catcher: Cover home plate.

First baseman: Become the cutoff man on the throw to the plate.

Second baseman: When convinced that the hit is at least a double, assume a trail position 20 feet behind the shortstop. Tell the shortstop whether to throw to third or home.

Shortstop: Assume the cutoff position, in line with home plate.

Third baseman: Cover third base.

Leftfielder: Back up the centerfielder.

Centerfielder: Field the ball and hit the cutoff man (shortstop).

Rightfielder: Back up the second-base area.

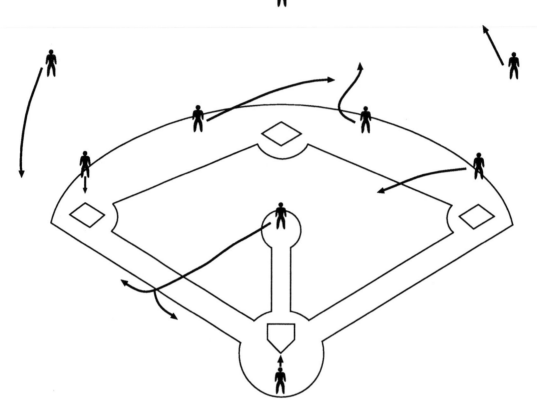

Sure double, possible triple, in the right-center-field gap—men on base

Pitcher: Go to a position halfway between home plate and third base, read the play, and back up the appropriate base.

Catcher: Cover home plate.

First baseman: Become the cutoff man on the throw to the plate.

Second baseman: Assume the cutoff position, in line with home plate.

Shortstop: When convinced that the hit is at least a double, assume a trail position 20 feet behind the second baseman. Tell the second baseman whether to throw to third or home.

Third baseman: Cover third base.

Leftfielder: Back up the third-base area.

Centerfielder: Field the ball and hit the cutoff man (second baseman).

Rightfielder: Back up the centerfielder.

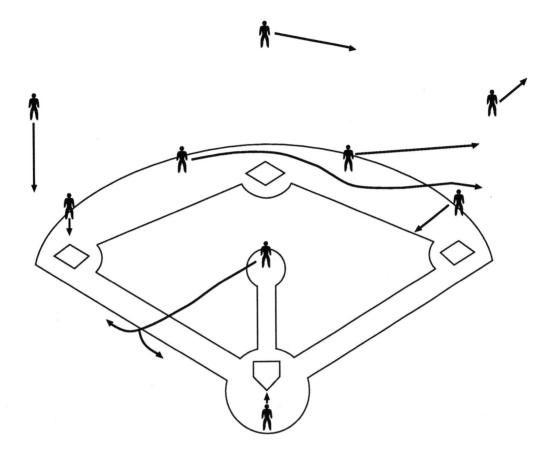

Sure double, possible triple, down the right-field line—men on base

Pitcher: Go to a position halfway between home plate and third base, read the play, and back up the appropriate base.

Catcher: Cover home plate.

First baseman: Become the cutoff man on the throw to the plate.

Second baseman: Assume the cutoff position, in line with home plate.

Shortstop: When convinced that the hit is at least a double, assume a trail position 20 feet behind the second baseman. Tell the second baseman where to throw the ball.

Third baseman: Cover third base.

Leftfielder: Back up the third-base area.

Centerfielder: Back up the rightfielder.

Rightfielder: Field the ball and hit the cutoff man (second baseman).

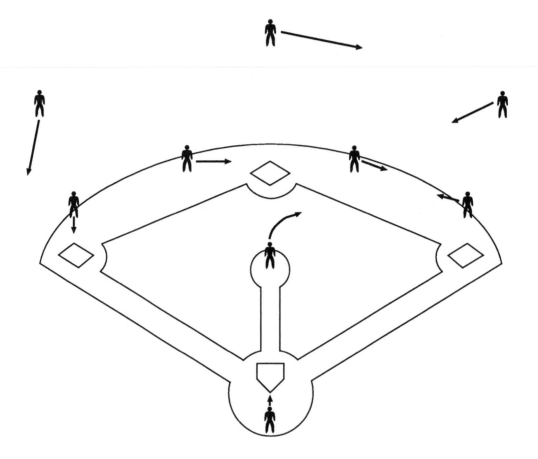

INFIELD POP FLIES

Pop fly to the right side of the infield—bases empty or men on base

Pitcher: Help direct traffic and reinforce the "I've got it" call.

Catcher: Cover home plate.

First baseman: When the ball gets to the top of its flight, call loudly if you want to make the catch; give way if the second baseman calls the ball. Remember, the rightfielder has priority over the infielders on this play.

Second baseman: When the ball gets to the top of its flight, call loudly if you want to make the catch; give way if the rightfielder calls the ball.

Shortstop: Cover second base.

Third baseman: Cover third base.

Leftfielder: Back up the third-base area.

Centerfielder: Back up the rightfielder.

Rightfielder: When the ball gets to the top of its flight, call loudly if you want to make the catch. Remember, you have priority on this catch.

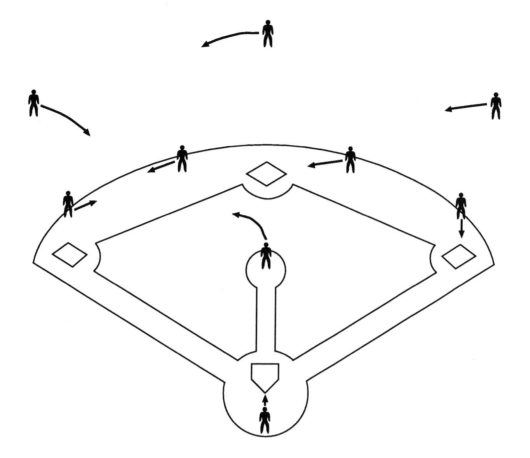

Pop fly to the left side of the infield—bases empty or men on base

Pitcher: Help direct traffic and reinforce the "I've got it" call.

Catcher: Cover home plate.

First baseman: Cover first base.

Second baseman: Cover second base.

Shortstop: When the ball gets to the top of its flight, call loudly if you want to make the catch; give way if the rightfielder calls the ball.

Third baseman: When the ball gets to the top of its flight, call loudly if you want to make the catch; give way if the shortstop calls the ball. Remember, the leftfielder has priority over the infielders on this play.

Leftfielder: When the ball gets to the top of its flight, call loudly if you want to make the catch. Remember, you have priority on this catch.

Centerfielder: Back up the leftfielder.

Rightfielder: Back up the second-base area.

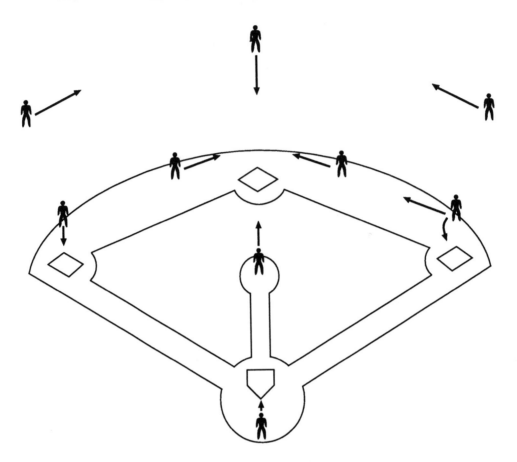

Pop fly to the middle of the infield—bases empty or men on base

Pitcher: Help direct traffic and reinforce the "I've got it" call. Remember, you may have to cover second base if both middle infielders go for the ball and the first baseman is not there to cover.

Catcher: Cover home plate.

First baseman: Cover second base if both middle infielders go for the ball; otherwise, cover first.

Second baseman: When the ball gets to the top of its flight, call loudly if you want to make the catch; give way if the centerfielder calls the ball. If the shortstop calls the ball early, retreat and cover second.

Shortstop: When the ball gets to the top of its flight, call loudly if you want to make the catch; give way if the centerfielder calls the ball. If the second baseman calls the ball early, retreat and cover second.

Third baseman: Cover third base.

Leftfielder: Back up the centerfielder.

Centerfielder: When the ball gets to the top of its flight, call loudly if you want to make the catch. Remember, you have priority on this catch.

Rightfielder: Back up the centerfielder.

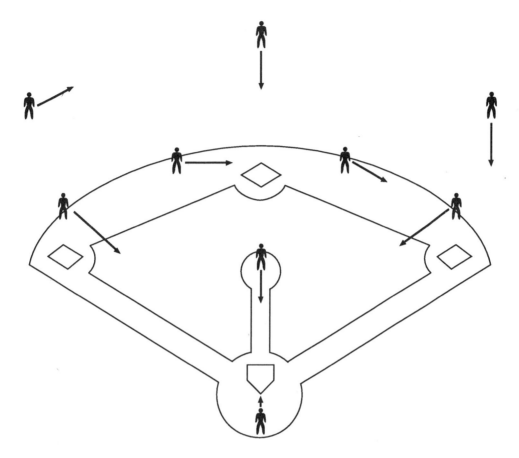

BUNT DEFENSES

Sacrifice bunt—runner on first base

Pitcher: Throw a strike, cover the middle of the infield, field the ball if necessary, listen for the catcher to direct the throw, and throw to the correct base.

Catcher: Direct the infielders as to where to throw the ball.

First baseman: Hold the runner on first; then charge and cover the right side of the infield, field the ball if necessary, listen for the catcher to direct the throw, and throw to the correct base.

Second baseman: Cover first base.

Shortstop: Cover second base.

Third baseman: Begin on the edge of the grass; then charge and cover the left side of the infield, field the ball if necessary, listen for the catcher to direct the throw, and throw to the correct base.

Leftfielder: Back up the centerfielder.

Centerfielder: Back up the possible throw to second base.

Rightfielder: Back up the possible throw to first base.

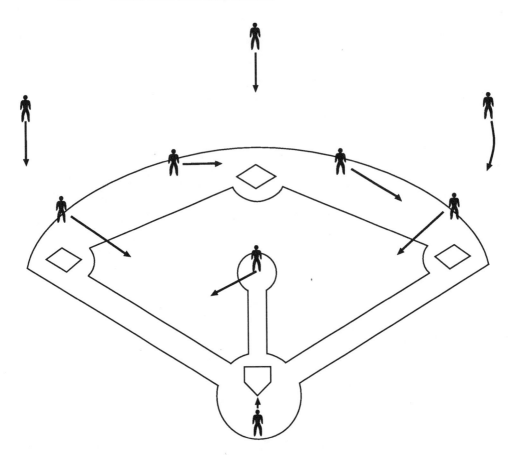

Sacrifice bunt—runners on first and second (standard coverage, designed to get the out at first)

Pitcher: Throw a strike, cover the third-base line, field the ball if necessary, listen for the catcher to direct the throw, and throw to the correct base.

Catcher: Direct the infielders as to where to throw the ball.

First baseman: Cover the right side of the infield, field the ball if necessary, listen for the catcher to direct the throw, and throw to the correct base.

Second baseman: Cover first base.

Shortstop: Cover second base.

Third baseman: Begin on the edge of the grass; then charge and cover the left side of the infield, field the ball if necessary (be aggressive and call the pitcher off the ball if necessary), listen for the catcher to direct the throw, and throw to the correct base.

Leftfielder: Back up the possible throw to third base.

Centerfielder: Back up the possible throw to second base.

Rightfielder: Back up the possible throw to first base.

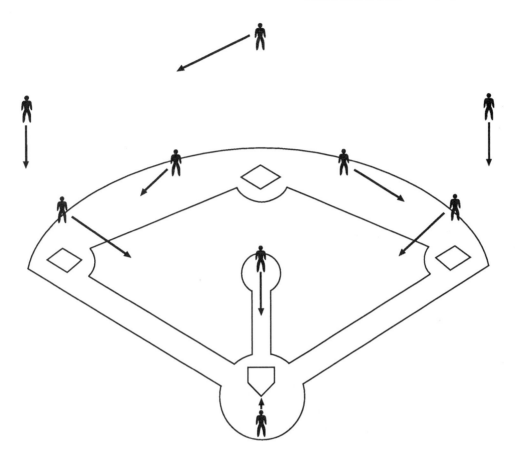

*Sacrifice bunt—runners on first and second (the wheel play,
designed to force the runner at third)*

Pitcher: Wait for the shortstop to break for third. Throw a strike, cover the middle of the infield, field the ball if necessary, listen for the catcher to direct the throw, and throw to the correct base (a force at third).

Catcher: Direct the infielders as to where to throw the ball (remember, there is nobody covering second on this play).

First baseman: Cover the right side of the infield, field the ball if necessary, listen for the catcher to direct the throw, and throw to the correct base.

Second baseman: Cover first base.

Shortstop: Position yourself behind the runner, just off his right shoulder; break to cover third when the pitcher reaches the set position.

Third baseman: Begin on the edge of the grass; then charge hard and cover the left side of the infield, field the ball if necessary (be aggressive and call the pitcher off the ball if necessary), listen for the catcher to direct the throw, and throw to the correct base (a force at third).

Leftfielder: Back up the possible throw to third base.

Centerfielder: Back up the leftfielder.

Rightfielder: Back up the possible throw to first base.

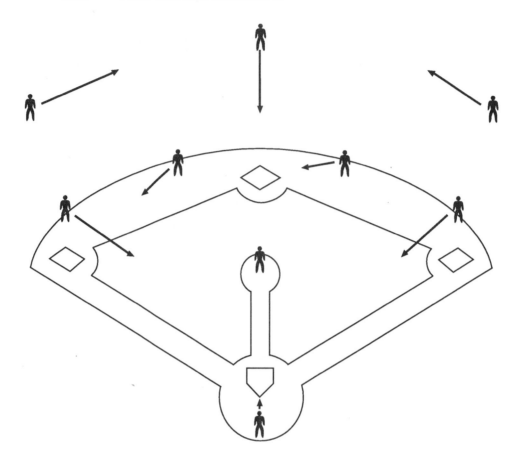

Sacrifice bunt in order—runners on first and second (pickoff play, designed to pick the runner off second)

Pitcher: Watch the shortstop break for third and throw to the second baseman for the pickoff.

Catcher: Cover home plate.

First baseman: Cover the right side of the infield, as in the wheel play.

Second baseman: Take a step toward first and then break to second for the pickoff.

Shortstop: Position yourself behind the runner, just off his right shoulder; break to cover third when the pitcher reaches the set position (although no pitch is thrown, you must break as if the wheel play were on).

Third baseman: Begin on the edge of the grass; then charge hard and cover the left side of the infield.

Leftfielder: Back up the centerfielder.

Centerfielder: Back up second base.

Rightfielder: Back up the centerfielder.

Note: Remember that this pickoff play must be disguised as the wheel play in order to fool the runner at second.

9
THE ATHLETIC MACHINE

When preparing for an activity it is always helpful to analyze the activity itself. The questions to be answered are: What is the nature of this activity? What demands does it place on the body? How can I best meet these demands?

Baseball is a game of short bursts of anaerobic activity. On the recreational level (one game a week), the sport simply does not require intensive conditioning. But at the higher levels ballplayers are expected to maintain optimum performance levels nearly every day for up to eight months. Obviously, conditioning needs must be much more clearly defined.

WEIGHT TRAINING FOR BASEBALL PLAYERS

Baseball has been the most reluctant of sports to become involved in modern training methods. Tradition held that weight lifting was bad because it would make a player "muscle-bound." It is ironic that these same old-time baseball people would comment that certain hitters were so strong that they could "knock the ball out of any park." This strength, although a product of genetic makeup, was probably enhanced by some form of weight training.

Major league trainer Dave Labossiere assisted in the preparation of this chapter.

In the old days, America was a more rural and less sedentary society. Professional ballplayers often developed their strength through manual labor—by lifting crates or perhaps bales of hay. Todays' weight-training programs must take the place of manual labor for strength enhancement.

It is important that any strength gain is *functional:* the player must be able to transfer the newly gained strength to the task at hand. For example, a hitter has to handle a bat that weighs as much as 35 ounces; and although strength is a factor, power is more important. Power is the product of both strength and speed. Therefore, the player must train for speed as well as pure strength.

I suggest using free weights for arm and shoulder work. Free weights require you to balance as well as lift the weight, thus strengthening the synergistic muscles—those smaller assisting muscles that facilitate control and coordination. As a result, strength gained from lifting is more easily transferred to specific skills because the muscles are used to working together. All fine motor skills, such as swinging a bat or throwing a ball, involve the use of synergistic muscles.

Weight machines, on the other hand, tend to keep the muscles too isolated and do most of the balancing for you, so the synergistic muscles aren't exercised as much. But machines are okay for lower-body work—most such motions in baseball involve large muscle movements that don't require high levels of skill. In addition, machines are safer to use, a factor that becomes more important as more weight is increased.

CONDITIONING FOR BASEBALL

Baseball is a sprinting game, and I believe that the only running that a player should do is sprinting. The sprint program should last between 20 and 30 minutes and should consist of one time period of work and two periods of rest. For example, if you are running 100-yard dashes in 12 seconds, the rest period between each sprint should be 24 seconds.

Stretching and warm-up are very important, but they are distinctly different activities. You stretch to increase range of motion and to help decrease your chance of injury; you warm up to prepare your body tissues for activity. It is always best to work on flexibility when you are already warmed up. I suggest jogging around the field, riding a bike, jumping rope, etc., to warm up and then easing into stretching exercises. When you arrive at the field to play a game, you should jog around the field twice and run several 30-yard dashes (easy at first); when you begin to perspire, stop and stretch or work on flexibility.

Upper-Body Workout

Body part	Action	Tool
Hands	Squeeze	Ball or putty
Forearms	Wrist curl—palm up	Dumbbell
	Wrist curl—palm down	
Biceps	Elbow curl	Dumbbell
Triceps	Elbow extension	Dumbbell
Shoulders	Lateral raise	Dumbbell
Chest	Push-ups with wide grip	Body weight
	Push-ups with narrow grip	
Back	Reverse butterfly	Dumbbell

Do 1 set of 50 repetitions for the hand exercise; for the rest, do 1 set of from 12 to 20 repetitions.

You will note the absence of the bench press, an exercise that has more potential liability than benefit for baseball players. No baseball activity requires a similar motion. The bench press can injure the posterior shoulder and tighten the anterior shoulder. Chest muscles can be toned with wide-grip push-ups, which can be intensified by putting the feet on a bench or chair. My advice is to avoid the bench press.

Rotator-Cuff Program

The rotator-cuff program is the most important group of exercises for baseball players. Please pay special attention to form; it is very important to do the motions exactly as demonstrated.

Exercise 1—Deltoid and Superspinatus

Stand with hands at side.

Lift hands forward with palms facing downward (lift only to shoulder level). Return hands to starting position.

Lift hands halfway between forward and straight out to the side with the thumb facing down (lift only to shoulder level). Return hands to starting position.

Lift hands straight out to the side with palms facing down. Return to starting position.

Lift hands straight up along side of body so that elbows point back and palms face body. Return to starting position.

Exercise 2—External Rotator

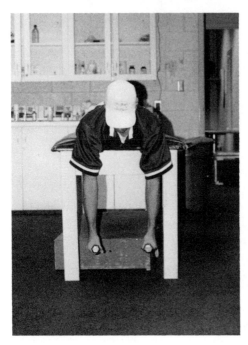 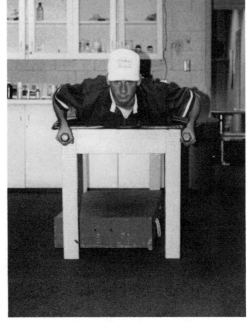

Hang hands straight down with palms facing each other.

Lift elbows straight up so that they form a straight line across the shoulders.

Rotate hands to table level.

Reverse the sequence and return to starting position.

Exercise 3—Rotator Cuff

 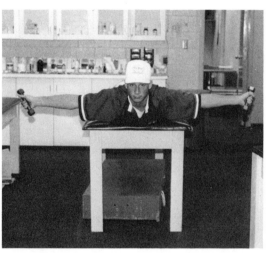

Hang arm over the edge of a table and rotate arm so that the thumb faces outward.

Lift arms straight away from the body with thumbs up.

Return to starting position.

Exercise 4—Posterior Deltoid

Same starting position as Exercise 3.

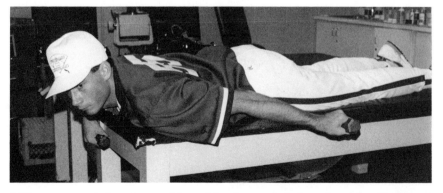

Lift arm straight along side of body to height of table. Return to starting position.

Exercise 5—Deltoid

Lift arms forward to shoulder height with palms facing down.	Move arms to right, keeping them extended and about the same distance apart. Do not move hips or trunk.

Swing arms back to left, keeping them apart.

Exercise 6—Negative External Rotation

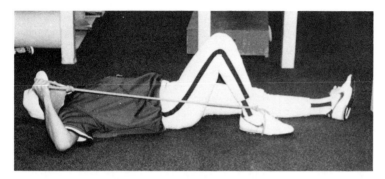

Lie on back and hook tube on foot; bend knee. Hold tube in hand (palm facing body). Bend elbow to 90 degrees.

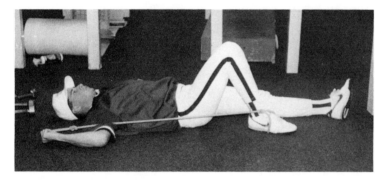

Hold arm at 90 degrees from body. Return to starting position.

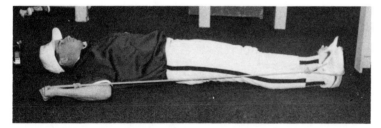

Rotate arm back (thumb should touch ground). Straighten leg.

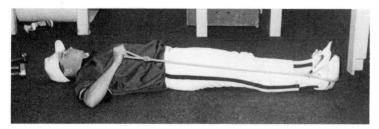

Slowly rotate inward as far as you can. Return to starting position.

These exercises are meant to be done slowly. For the first five you should begin with no weight and 1 set of 8 repetitions. Add 2 repetitions every week until you get to 20 repetitions. Then go to 5 pounds and 1 set of 8 repetitions and once again build to 20 repetitions. For Exercise 6 surgical tubing works the best; it is available in most hospital supply stores and some pharmacies. Always do 1 set of 10 reps of this exercise. Simply add resistance by shortening the tube.

It is strongly suggested that you do these exercises in the order given because it exercises the muscle groups in the most efficient way. By following this program, you can virtually eliminate arm injuries. With proper weight training and good throwing mechanics, you can improve your velocity, sometimes in as little as three months.

Lower-Body Workout

Body Part	Action	Tool
Knee	Squats and Lunges	Body weight
Calf	Toe raises	Body weight
Groin	Side leg lifts	Leg weight

Do 1 set of 25 repetitions for each of these lower-body exercises.

This entire conditioning program should be performed three days a week or every other day; always give yourself a day of rest between workout days.

10
COLLEGE AND PROFESSIONAL BASEBALL

COLLEGE BASEBALL

Ballplayers are evaluated at every level of baseball—from Little League tryouts to major league games, they are always under a microscope. When players get to the high school level this process intensifies as college and pro scouts begin to take notice.

Players should never select a college or university solely because of its baseball program. I know kids who have gone to certain colleges because they like the field, or the uniforms, or the road trips that the team makes. Sure, college baseball is fun and those things might add to the fun, but *you are attending college for an education.*

College scholarships are not readily available and, in fact, are quite rare for baseball players. Even the major college baseball programs have few scholarships of any kind to offer, and only the most highly recruited players get full scholarships. These players will usually get lots of attention from professional scouts and are sometimes drafted in the higher rounds by major league baseball. Getting a free education by playing baseball sounds wonderful, but the truth is getting any financial help at all is unusual for the average player.

Hundreds of kids a year enroll in the so-called baseball schools, only to wash out after an unfair tryout of some kind. Coaches at Division I schools know who will start for them each year, and walk-ons rarely get much more than a token look. At some high-powered programs, two or three hundred kids come out for baseball, and the coaching staff goes through them quickly out of necessity. Players must produce in a hurry or they are cut.

There are some exceptions, however: Eric Karros was a hitting student at the San Diego School of Baseball for years, was a walk-on at UCLA, and as a member of the Los Angeles Dodgers was named the National League's Rookie of the Year.

Players who go away to school often come back unhappy. At age 18, most kids are not ready to go away from home and face the pressure of college life. Freshmen drop out or fail by the hundreds at most universities, and it takes a lot of hard work just to succeed in college even without the pressures of playing sports. I recommend going to school close to home (no more than a couple of hours' drive), at least during the first two years. Young people need a support system, and parents and friends can make the difference in educational success.

The junior colleges offer better opportunities for kids with average or slightly above average ability to play and gain experience. For the player who loves to play and needs the experience, playing at a junior college as a freshman is much better than playing on a junior varsity at a four-year school. Most junior varsity programs at four-year schools are very weak. They are coached by graduate assistants with little or no coaching experience, and they play a short schedule against weak opponents. After a player plays well at a junior college, the college recruiters will come around.

College baseball is a wonderful experience—I highly recommend it for everyone. At most colleges, players get good coaching—sometimes even better than in professional baseball. College baseball teams for the most part play "little ball": they play for one run at a time. This kind of baseball teaches you the game. When you constantly move runners, hit-and-run, sacrifice bunt, and play tight defense against all of these strategies, you are really learning to play the game. I think that some college coaches overdo this a bit, but basically they do a great job of teaching unselfish team play.

PROFESSIONAL BASEBALL AND SCOUTING

I don't like to see high school players sign professional contracts. The sad truth is that only 5 percent of signed players ever play a day in the major leagues. Less than 1 percent have long successful major league careers. With these kinds of odds facing players, an education is a must. I have seen hundreds of players come back home after two seasons, released from their pro contracts and unable to play college ball with their buddies. Their bonus is sometimes already gone on taxes and a new car. I know that this is not a popular philosophy in the business of professional baseball, but anyone who truly cares about kids would not endorse a professional career beginning at age 17 or 18. After playing college baseball, players are simply better equipped to handle the pressure and the lifestyle of pro ball.

Most professional scouts don't pay much attention to players' performances—things like batting average and earned-run average shouldn't matter much to a good scout. When a scout is doing his job properly, he is evaluating the physical tools of the players that he is watching. Scouts are interested in running speed, bat speed and power, and arm strength in position players. In pitchers they are looking for control, fastball velocity, and sharpness of breaking pitches.

Most scouts also pay close attention to a player's attitude toward the game and his teammates as well as his general character. It is important to draft and sign players who love baseball. It might sound funny, but many players with physical tools don't make it because they don't enjoy playing baseball. With a 200-game schedule (counting spring training), a player had better like the game a lot.

Scouts who cover the high schools and colleges are either full-time or part-time. The part-time scouts, called "bird dogs," recommend players to the "area" (full-time) scouts and receive a commission if the player makes it to the majors. If the area scout likes a player and thinks that he can eventually play in the majors, he recommends to the scouting supervisor that the organization consider him for the draft. The supervisor often will call in a national "cross-checker" to evaluate the player and file a report. If they agree that the player will eventually become a major leaguer, they will try to draft the player the following June.

WHO IS A PROSPECT?

Scouts are called upon to evaluate a player's physical tools as they see them today and look into their crystal ball and tell the organization that is paying them what that player will look like three to five years in the future. It is no wonder that there are so many horror stories of high schoolers who are washed up at age 19 or 20 with no college eligibility left. Some scouts work 20 years without ever signing a player who becomes a good major leaguer. Scouting and evaluating free-agent (high school and college) talent is the single hardest thing to do in professional baseball.

Sometimes scouts can't get the players they want. In the early 1980s Reggie Waller, who was at that time scouting for the Houston Astros, was very enthusiastic about signing a young outfielder at San Diego State University. However, the Astros had given up their first two draft choices in order to sign Don Sutton and Dave Roberts. Before Reggie had a chance the San Diego Padres drafted the player in the third round. The outfielder's name? Tony Gwynn.

So what is it that players must have to be signed or to have college baseball coaches offer them scholarships? College coaches are looking for people who are good players right now and can help their programs in the very near future. Professional scouts don't ignore players who are good now but are on the lookout for players with "projectability"—that is, players who have the physical tools to become great players in the future given enough time, instruction, and experience. Many major league stars were not the best player on their high school or college teams.

For position players, physical tools are evaluated as an entire package. In other words, if the bat is evaluated highly, then arm strength is not regarded as a big factor; if the bat is weak, then the defensive skills and speed have to be much better. The old line "If you swing the bat, they will find a place for you" is still very true today.

All players are graded based on the following scale:

8—outstanding
7—way above average
6—above average
5—average
4—just below average
3—way below average
2—poor
1—very poor

Each skill is broken down into both a present grade and a future grade. For example, if a shortstop gets a grade of 5 (present) and 6 (future) for his arm strength, this means that his arm is considered to be as strong as that of the average major league shortstop playing in the big leagues today, and it is projected to be above average sometime in the future. In order for a position player to be judged an average major league runner, he would have to go to first base in 4.4 seconds from the right side of the plate and 4.2 seconds from the left side. After the scout grades each individual skill, he combines the scores and comes up with an O.F.P. number ("overall future potential") that helps rank the player in the draft.

PLAYING PROFESSIONAL BASEBALL

Playing professional baseball is the opportunity of a lifetime. Of the thousands of players eligible for the draft each year only 700 or so sign contracts and go out and play. I hope that every player who gets this chance realizes how lucky he is.

Most players begin their careers at the rookie league or Class-A levels. Once in a while, a college junior or senior will be sent to the Double-A level to begin his pro baseball career. Generally speaking, players move up one notch at a time as they perform to the levels set by each organization. Higher draft choices will usually move up quickly unless they have a very tough time competing. In the lower minors, being broke and riding buses becomes a way of life. Even now, the players make less than a thousand dollars a month (just for a five-month season), and times are hard.

After three or four years in pro ball, a player is eligible to be drafted by other clubs in what is called the "rule 5" draft, held at the annual winter meetings. This is the time when a club may elect to place a player on the major league roster to "protect" itself from losing him to another team. Once on a major league roster, a player starts to make a little money for the first time. In order to make the major league minimum salary, he must make the major league club's 25-man squad. The roster of a major league club remains at 25 from opening day until September 1; on that date the club may add any or all of the players on its roster (up to 40) to the active list.

As the average major league salary approaches $1,000,000 a year, more and more athletes are realizing that baseball is the sport to play. Professional baseball is no longer losing the premium athletes to other sports as it used to. Athletes of every size can play baseball, and in the warmer climates they can play twelve months a year.

I have made $500 a month, received $3 a day in meal money, stayed in terrible hotels, ridden on a bus for 15 hours at a time, lived with seven other guys, and survived on peanut butter and jelly, and you know what? I loved it. Getting paid to play baseball is the greatest thing that could ever happen to someone who loves the game as I do. Everything I have in life I owe to professional baseball.

INDEX

Sliding, 154–55, 158–59
Spilt-fingered fastball, 28–30
Squeeze, 7, 54
Stances (hitting), 163–66
Starting position, 69
Stealing bases. *See* Basestealing
Striking out, 182
Sun, 138–40
Swing, 168–73

T
Tagging, 77–79, 118–21
Tension, 11–12
Third base, 6–7, 99
3-6-3 double play, 97–98
Throwing (catcher), 109–18
    first and third double steal, 117
    pitchouts, 110
    pickoffs at first base, 110
    throwing to second, 110–14
    throwing to third, 114–15

Throwing (outfield), 131–35
    and catching fly balls, 133–34
    "drifting" to the ball, 135
    drill, 134
    and fielding ground balls, 131
Tracking the ball, 174–76
Turns, 144
Two-seam grip, 27–28

U
Umpires, 2
Upper-body workout, 233
Uppercut, 183–86

V
Videotape, 3
Visualization, 12–13

W
Weight training, 221–22
Winning, 1–2